contents

introduction

Barbecues are not only a delicious way of cooking food outside and an interesting alternative to a picnic, they are also healthy and fun. Whether you are cooking a small weekend lunch for the family or throwing a summer party for 20 guests, a barbecue can provide plenty of variety and entertainment for everyone. Let your guests or the family join in and help to cook and serve their own food – even the children can help if they are supervised by an adult.

The idea of a barbecue is very ancient and spans many cultures. Although meat is the traditional staple, vegetarians can also enjoy a wide variety of barbecued dishes. This book features traditional 'sausage sizzle' barbecue dishes, as well as more exotic and unusual ones. You can begin by cooking simple barbecues, such as sausages, hamburgers and steaks, until you build up your confidence and become more familiar with your barbecue. When you feel that you are ready to try something more complicated, experiment with meats, vegetables, marinades and a range of different dishes. You can even practise cooking these dishes under the grill in your kitchen before serving them from the barbecue at a party. Virtually any type of food can be cooked on a barbecue, from meat, poultry and seafood to vegetables, tofu and desserts. You can make kebabs on skewers, use lean cuts of meat with some seasoning, make foil parcels or try out your own ideas. Barbecues are immensely versatile. Try serving a choice of different foods with your main dishes. Baked potatoes and salads are the traditional accompaniments to serve at a barbecue, but you can liven these up. Place bowls of different fillings on the table for your guests to have with their baked potatoes – tuna and mayonnaise, creamy cheeses or a spicy sweetcorn relish. It is very easy to add interest to a barbecue. Try a selection of salads – a green salad for traditionalists and a pasta, rice, tomato or mixed bean salad to add colour and extra flavour.

Sweet dishes can also be cooked on the barbecue – simply wrap them in foil parcels to keep them away from meat juices. This also works brilliantly if you have vegetarian guests who will not like their vegetables to come into contact with the meat you are cooking.

Try a barbecue birthday party for children, depending on their ages. If you have very young children, it may be safer to keep them away from the barbecue altogether. However, if your children are older, they can help you to choose the menu and prepare and even cook some of the dishes. A barbecue also adds a delightful twist to an ordinary garden party and children will love it.

Most cuisines throughout the world have at least one dish that is wonderful cooked on a barbecue. This book features recipes from across the globe – Caribbean dishes, such as Caribbean Fish Kebabs (see page 16), Jamaican Kebabs (see page 56) and Jerk Chicken (see page 61), and spicy Cajun dishes, such as the traditional Cajun Chicken (see page 52) and the more unusual Cajun Vegetables (see page 147). You can try the Mexican Tuna (see page 30) or Greek Red Mullet Parcels (see page 33) if you are a seafood lover. There is spicy Thai Chicken (see page 62) for those who like an Asian flavour to their food and Chicken Tikka (see page 72) for those who prefer an Indian influence. Fruity Duck (see page 82) and Butterflied Poussins (see page 84) are impressive dishes for entertaining guests, while Best-ever Burgers (see page 90) and an Easy Mixed Grill (see page 122) are simpler ones for when you have less time or

barbecue

100 BEST RECIPES

LINDA DOESER

p

This is a Parragon Book
First published in 2003

Parragon
Queen Street House
4 Queen Street
Bath BA1 1HE
United Kingdom

Created and produced by
The Bridgewater Book Company Ltd,
Lewes, East Sussex

Photographer Ian Parsons
Home economists Sara Hesketh and Richard Green

ISBN: 0–75259–935–6

Printed in China

NOTE

This book uses metric and imperial measurements. Follow the same units
of measurement throughout; do not mix metric and imperial. All spoon
measurements are level: teaspoons are assumed to be 5 ml and tablespoons
are assumed to be 15 ml. Unless otherwise stated, milk is assumed to be full fat,
eggs and individual vegetables such as potatoes are medium, and pepper
is freshly ground black pepper.

The times given for each recipe are an approximate guide only
because the preparation times may differ according to the techniques used
by different people and the cooking times may vary as a result of the type of
barbecue used, the size and type of grill, the heat level and the weather
conditions. The preparation times include chilling and
marinating times, where appropriate.

The nutritional information provided for each recipe is per serving
or per portion. Optional ingredients, variations or serving suggestions
have not been included in the calculations.

Recipes using raw or very lightly cooked eggs should be avoided
by infants, the elderly, pregnant women, convalescents, and anyone
suffering from an illness.

energy. There are dishes to suit every palate – Indonesian Beef Kebabs (see page 100) for a meat-lover willing to experiment and Mushroom Burgers (see page 139) for vegetarians with a hearty appetite.

You can serve a dessert as simple as vanilla ice cream, or a grilled one, such as Barbecued Fruit with Maple Syrup (see page 172) or Banana Sizzles (see page 173), as a perfect finale to any barbecue.

types of barbecue

There are many different types of barbecue available and you are sure to find one to suit your specific needs, depending on size and how often you are likely to use it. If you have only one barbecue every summer, it may be sensible just to buy a disposable grill.

When choosing a barbecue, be sure to look around. as there is a large range and the prices can vary drastically. Bear in mind how many people you are likely to be cooking for and how large your garden is. Will the smoke annoy your neighbours? Should you consider a built-in brick barbecue? How much would you like to spend? What sort of fuel would you prefer to use? Plan the type of barbecue you will need for your lifestyle.

- You can make your own barbecue, whether permanent or temporary. Use the materials around you, on the beach, at a picnic or in your garden. A pile of stones or bricks with small pieces of wood as fuel works well with a rack placed over the top.

- Disposable barbecues are usually little more than a foil tray with a rack resting near the top and this is adequate for a small picnic or lunch. They are inexpensive and the fuel supplied as part of the pack will last for about 1 hour. They can be used only once.

- Portable barbecues vary in size and price and are a popular choice. They are light and easy to carry and fold away to fit into a car boot. These are ideal for a larger picnic where you will not have to walk too far. They are especially easy to clean.

- Brazier barbecues are another popular choice and are portable to a limited extent. Although you could not transport a brazier barbecue to a picnic, it can easily be moved into a shed for storage or to another part of the garden. Some brazier barbecues have legs while others have wheels, but do make sure that the height is convenient for the person who will be doing most of the cooking, as they can sometimes be a little low. If your garden is windy, a brazier may not be the best choice since these are open barbecues, although many do have a hood to offer some protection. Some have shelves attached to the side, which are useful for storing cooking utensils.

- Hibachi barbecues are small and easy to transport. They originate from Japan, where the name translates as 'firebox'. They are inexpensive and are now usually made from lightweight materials, although they are traditionally made from cast iron.

- Kettle-grill barbecues are versatile and efficient and you can also use them with the lid on for smoking foods. The large lid offers protection from the wind and can rescue a barbecue party if the weather is unfavourable. Many have a spit attachment. Joints of meat or whole chickens can be cooked on this type of barbecue and they are large enough for most families. Meat cooks evenly and it is easy to control the heat using the air vents. These are the best choice for people who do not want a built-in barbecue.

- Gas and electric barbecues are very efficient and you do not have to wait for the coals to heat up, as it takes only 10 minutes for them to warm up. They are a good choice if you are planning to use your barbecue commercially – they tend to be expensive. They are easy to operate, but do not produce the traditional smoky flavour of grilling over charcoal.

- Permanent barbecues are an excellent choice if you plan to barbecue frequently. They can be built to the right size for your family and do not have to be expensive. Firstly, go out into your garden and choose the best site for your barbecue. It should be a little distance from the house and from your neighbours, but close to the kitchen if possible. You can build your barbecue with simple materials, such as house bricks, but the bricks inside should be firebricks that can withstand the intense heat. You can put a metal grilling rack at whatever height you want – adjustable if you like – and a metal tray for the fuel. You can also purchase packs containing everything you will need.

types of fuel

There are different types of fuel for different types of barbecue and you should consider which type you would prefer to use before buying your barbecue. If you do not feel happy using charcoal or wood, a gas or electric barbecue may be what you need. Be careful to store your fuel in a dry place, whatever type you use.

- Lumpwood charcoal is easy to ignite, but will burn relatively quickly. It is readily available and inexpensive.
- Charcoal briquettes can take a while to ignite, but they burn for a long time with little smell or smoke. They are ideal for a small garden where the barbecue is near windows and other people's houses.
- Self-igniting charcoal is lumpwood charcoal or briquettes that have been coated with a flammable chemical, which will light very easily. You should wait until the chemical has burnt off before adding food to the barbecue, as it may give off an undesirable smell, which can taint the food.
- Hardwoods can be used for barbecues. Woods such as oak and apple are best, as they burn slowly and have a pleasant smell. Softwoods are not appropriate, as they burn too fast and will spark. If you are going to use wood as a fuel, remember that it will need constant attention to maintain an even heat. Be careful to keep wood supplies away from the barbecue as flying sparks could ignite them.

- Wood chips and herbs are designed to be added to the fire, not used as a main fuel. Depending on what you are cooking, sprigs of rosemary, thyme and sage make particularly attractive additions to a barbecue and will give off a delicious aroma. Scatter them over the hot coals or wood underneath the food.

getting going

Lighting a barbecue need not be a worry and an effort. It should take only a few minutes, providing that you prepare well and make sure that you have extra fuel nearby. Always follow the instructions that come with the fuel if you are using self-igniting charcoal. Follow these steps for a successful barbecue.

1 Use foil to line the base of your barbecue underneath the fire grate. This will make cleaning easier and will keep the bottom of the barbecue hot.

2 Spread a layer of whichever fuel you are using on to the fire grate. Small pieces at the bottom and medium-sized pieces on top of them works best. The layer of charcoal or wood should be 5-cm/2-inches deep and resemble a pyramid in the centre of the grate.

3 Using firelighter cubes and liquid is most effective, but you should be able to light your barbecue with just one or the other. If using firelighter cubes, place one or two cubes in the centre of the pyramid. If using liquid firelighter, pour a few tablespoons into the fuel and leave for a minute. Light the barbecue using a long match or taper and leave for 15 minutes. Spread the coals into an even layer and leave for 40 minutes, or until they are covered with a thin layer of grey ash and are hot enough to begin cooking. Spread the hot coals at least 2.5 cm/1 inch further than the area on which you will be cooking the food.

Never add petrol, lighter fluid or other flammable materials to a barbecue.

4 To control the heat of the barbecue once the coals are hot enough for cooking, raise or lower the grill rack. If your barbecue has air vents, open these to raise the temperature of the barbecue and close them to lower it. You can also push the hot coals carefully into the centre of the barbecue to provide a higher heat in the middle and a lower heat nearer the edges, where you can put food once it is cooked.

safety

Barbecuing is a safe way of cooking as long as you use your common sense. Try not to be over-ambitious if you have not used a barbecue before and always err on the side of caution.

- Make sure that your barbecue is stable and on a flat surface before you light it. Once it is lit, do not move it.

- Keep the barbecue away from trees and shrubs and cut back a shrub instead of moving the barbecue. Note which way the wind is blowing before lighting the barbecue.

- Never add any flammable liquids to try to speed up the ignition of the barbecue. Only ever use fuels designed for the purpose, such as firelighter cubes and liquid. Remember that some fuels take time to build up heat.

- Use only the recommended types of fuel on your barbecue, following any instructions that came with it. Some fuels are not appropriate for some types of barbecue.

- Always have a bucket of water nearby in case the fire gets out of control. If your barbecue has a lid, this will also help to control the flames.

- Fat dripping from meat will make the coals flare up and can cause flames to get out of control. Trim excess fats from meats and shake or scrape off any excess marinade before adding to the barbecue.

- To avoid salmonella, listeria and food poisoning, always make sure that meat is cooked through. Pay attention in particular to chicken, turkey, pork and sausages. The cooked meat should have no pink flesh and the juices should run clear (not pink) when the meat is pierced through the thickest part with a skewer or the point of a sharp knife.

- If it is a particularly hot day, keep perishable foods in the refrigerator until it is time to serve them. Alternatively, you can store them outside in a cool bag with ice packs. Foods that can go off quickly and make people ill include meat, yogurt and mayonnaise.
- Do not reheat poultry once it has cooled. This rule includes putting food back on the barbecue if it has cooled down. When you serve your meal, try to make sure that the meat is thoroughly cooked through; if not, return to a hot barbecue before it cools down.
- Keep salads and cooked foods away from raw meat and wash your hands carefully after handling raw meat. Use different chopping boards, serving plates and utensils for raw meats.
- Keep pets away from food and the barbecue to avoid contamination and accidents. Cover food with netting or clean tea towels to keep insects away. Do not use the same tea towel to cover raw meat and then salad.
- Keep children away from the barbecue and teach them about the dangers of playing too close. Always have another adult nearby to supervise the children when you are cooking.
- Do not use a barbecue when you have been drinking alcohol and keep any strong alcoholic drinks away from the barbecue, as they can be flammable.
- Use utensils with long handles and make sure you have a range of tools handy so you do not leave the barbecue unattended. Keep oven gloves nearby.

tools and equipment

Oven gloves are useful to have, as the barbecue may become very hot after a while. Kebab skewers can burn your fingers, even if they are made of wood or bamboo. Plastic utensils should be avoided, as the intense heat from the barbecue can melt them. Metal utensils are best, but remember that they can get very hot. Buy good-quality utensils – a range of different ones will be useful, especially long-handled spoons, forks and fish slices designed specifically for barbecues. Include a pair of tongs, a brush or spoon for basting meat, and something for scraping stuck-on marinades and pieces of food off the grill. If you are using kebab skewers, metal ones can be rubbed with a piece of kitchen paper with some oil on it to stop the food from sticking. Bamboo and wooden skewers should be soaked in cold water for at least 30 minutes before using to prevent them burning. Wire fish baskets are useful extras, as they enable you to turn whole fish without the risk of it breaking up. They are available in a variety of styles and sizes. Brush with oil before using.

barbecue foods

You can begin by cooking a basic barbecue with traditional ingredients, such as sausages, hamburgers, drumsticks, chops and steaks. Simple foods like these are often best for children and large groups. Sausages are usually quite fatty, so prick them with a fork before cooking to stop them splitting, but watch for too much fat running on to the hot coals and causing flames to shoot up. Hamburgers can be made easily at home. You should prepare foods no more than a day before you are going to cook them, although foods such as hamburgers and sausages can be frozen. Thaw all meats thoroughly before cooking.

Steaks are very easy to cook and many guests will enjoy cooking their own. However, do make sure there are not too many people around the barbecue. Trim off any visible fat from the steak before cooking, as this will make it healthier and stop the fat from dripping on to the hot coals. Chops should be prepared in the same way and need to be cooked for quite a long time, especially if they have a bone. Pork chops should be especially well cooked – 15–20 minutes for a chop 2.5-cm/1-inch thick – and check to make sure that they are cooked through.

Many different types of fish can be cooked on a barbecue, from succulent salmon or tuna steaks to whole sardines and mackerel fillets. If you are going to cook fish steaks, select cuts that are of a uniform thickness, as these will cook more evenly. Try salmon steaks sprinkled with lemon juice and herbs or served with dill butter. Fish steaks have a tendency to fall apart and are often best cooked in foil parcels, which keep them moist and protect them from burning. Fish kebabs work very well, but be sure to choose a fish, such as cod or monkfish, that will hold together well – there is nothing more annoying than watching your food break apart and disappear into the coals at the bottom of the barbecue. Cod is ideal for kebabs and will go well with a strongly flavoured or spicy marinade. Oily fish, such as sardines or mackerel, will cook well on the barbecue and will not dry out.

Remember to be careful about washing your hands and cooking utensils between handling raw meats and other ingredients – for example, do not add a knob of butter to cooking chicken and use the same knife to spread butter on a roll. Remember to use separate chopping boards for meat and vegetables and do not put cooked meat near raw meat. Store foods out of direct sunlight and keep them chilled for as long as possible before cooking. Be especially aware when cooking food for young children, pregnant women or the elderly, as they are particularly susceptible to food poisoning, which can have serious effects. Chicken and raw eggs may contain salmonella, and mayonnaise and other egg-based dressings should be treated as carefully as raw meat.

cooking times

It is difficult to give precise times for cooking food on the barbecue, but this guide offers a rough idea. Before you begin cooking, you should make sure that the barbecue is very hot and that the grill rack is at the correct height. An easy way to gauge the heat is to hold out your hand slightly above the grill rack. If you can keep it there for only 2–3 seconds, the barbecue is hot enough to sear meat – any longer and it is not hot enough. Most foods, such as steaks and burgers, will need to be turned once or twice during cooking, but sausages and kebabs need to be turned frequently to ensure that they are evenly cooked. Do not leave food cooking unattended.

beef

- Steaks 2.5-cm/1-inch thick should be cooked over hot coals for 8 minutes. Cook for 5 minutes if you prefer steak rare, and for 12 minutes if you prefer it well done.
- Burgers 2-cm/¾-inch thick should be cooked over hot coals for 6–8 minutes.
- Kebabs made with medium-sized pieces of beef should be cooked for 7 minutes over hot coals.

lamb

- Leg steaks should be cooked over medium hot coals for 10–15 minutes. If they are thicker than 2 cm/ ¾ inch, increase the cooking time or use a meat mallet to tenderize and flatten them a little.
- Chops 2.5-cm/1-inch thick are best cooked over medium hot coals for 15 minutes.
- Kebabs made with 2.5-cm/1-inch cubes of lamb should be cooked for about 8–15 minutes over medium hot coals.

pork

- Cook chops for 15–20 minutes over medium hot coals and make sure that they are cooked through. If they are thicker than 2.5 cm/1 inch, increase the cooking time accordingly.
- Kebabs made with 2.5-cm/1-inch cubes of pork should be cooked for about 15 minutes over medium hot coals.
- Most pork spareribs are quite thick and will need to be cooked over medium hot coals for 40 minutes to ensure that they are cooked thoroughly.
- Thick sausages will need 10 minutes over medium hot coals; thinner ones may be ready slightly earlier.

chicken

- Quarters, legs and breasts with a bone should be cooked for 35 minutes over medium hot coals.

- Cook chicken drumsticks for 25–35 minutes over medium hot coals until the juices run clear, not pink, when you pierce the thickest part of the leg with a skewer or the point of a knife. If the drumsticks are very large, increase the cooking time.

- Whole breasts will need to be cooked over medium to hot coals for 15–20 minutes.

- Kebabs made with 2.5-cm/1-inch cubes of chicken should be cooked through after 10 minutes over medium hot coals.

fish and seafood

- Whole large fish can be cooked on a barbecue, if cooked over a low to medium heat. Allow 10 minutes per 2.5-cm/1-inch thickness.

- Cook whole small fish, up to 900 g/2 lb, for 14–20 minutes over medium to hot coals.

- Whole sardines should be cooked over medium to hot coals for 5–7 minutes.

- Fish steaks, such as salmon or tuna, or fish fillets up to 2.5-cm/1-inch thick, should be cooked for 6–10 minutes over medium hot coals.

- Fish kebabs made with 2.5-cm/1-inch cubes of fish should be cooked over medium hot coals for 7 minutes.

- Prawns in their shells should be cooked over medium hot coals for 7 minutes if they are large. Smaller prawns should be threaded on to kebab skewers. Large shelled prawns will cook slightly faster.

- Scallops or mussels in their shells should be cooked over medium hot coals until they open. Discard any scallops or mussels that do not open. Shelled and skewered seafood should be cooked for 7 minutes over medium hot coals.

spit-roasting

If you are lucky enough to have a roasting spit on your barbecue, you will find it invaluable when cooking for large numbers of guests. If you have parties regularly in summer and already have a barbecue, you will save time and effort by spit-roasting dishes. You can just put the meat on the spit and leave it to cook, while you spend most of your time with your guests. If you have a large family, a roasting spit can offer a healthy and filling alternative to a roast dinner. Baste the meat frequently while it is cooking to ensure an evenly cooked and succulent result.

- Joints of beef, such as rump or sirloin, up to about 1.5 kg/3 lb 5 oz will cook very well on a spit and will take 2–3 hours, depending on their size.

- A rolled shoulder of lamb weighing about 1.5 kg/ 3 lb 5 oz will cook in 1–1½ hours, depending on how well done you like it.

- Shoulder or loin joints of pork weighing about 1.5 kg/3 lb 5 oz will take 2–3 hours to cook through. Test with a skewer or the point of a sharp knife.

- Whole chickens weighing up to 1.5 kg/3 lb 5 oz will take 1¼ hours to cook. Test with a skewer or the point of a sharp knife, as they can take longer.

- Whole ducklings weighing up to 2.25 kg/5 lb are very fatty and take 1–1½ hours to cook.

hints and tips

The key to a successful barbecue is planning. It helps to know roughly how many people are coming, but if you are expecting a large number of guests, without knowing how many, make a good supply of basics, such as burgers, to be sure everyone has enough to eat. Most dishes freeze well and you can cook them under a conventional grill when you need them later.

You can make dishes for your barbecue well in advance. Make and freeze sausages, kebabs and burgers, although fish kebabs tend not to freeze well. Remove from the freezer 24 hours in advance and thaw in the refrigerator. Make salads in the morning, but avoid chopping ingredients that bruise or brown, such as avocado. Add dressings just before serving or put in a bowl at the table, as adding them to your salads too early will cause them to go soggy.

When you have lit the barbecue, you can begin to bring the meat outside. Brush the grill rack with a little sunflower oil to stop food sticking, being careful not to drip too much oil on to the hot coals.

Don't try to cook too much on the grill rack at once, as the food will not cook through or evenly. Try to cook the same types of food at the same time to avoid contamination. The coals should cover an area wider than that of the food, so even the edges of the grill rack should be quite hot. Use the edges to cook foods that require a lower heat to save having to let the barbecue cool down.

If you are cooking for vegetarian guests as well as meat-eaters, you may have to think about your barbecue a little more carefully. Vegetarian dishes should not be cooked on the same grill as meat dishes – you can keep a separate grill for vegetarians, although it is not fair to expect them to wait until everybody else's food is ready. You could also buy a disposable barbecue to cook only vegetable dishes. The easiest solution is to serve vegetarians with foil parcels of mixed beans, vegetables and cheese with a dressing. These parcels keep foods separate during cooking, can be cooked on the same grill as meat and are delicious. You could make a lot of these and serve them to meat-eaters as a side dish. For vegetarians, provide a choice of foods such as a selection of kebabs, parcels, salads and baked potatoes.

Foil parcels are often the best solution for cooking desserts. The simplest dessert and one popular with children is marshmallows toasted over the cooling coals, but this must be closely supervised. You can buy a disposable barbecue or use a separate rack, but wash utensils that have been used for savoury dishes.

Try to plan the menu so that there is something for everyone. There may be vegetarian guests, fussy children or meat-eaters not keen on salads, so offer a range of dishes. Remember to have a main vegetable to go with meat or fish. Foil-wrapped baked potatoes cooked on the barbecue are the easiest. Preheat the oven to 200°C/400°F/Gas Mark 6 and cook the potatoes for 30 minutes, before transferring to the barbecue, as they can take a long time to cook. Fresh rolls are also a good idea.

Offer a choice of drinks, alcoholic and non-alcoholic. Fruit punch with little or no alcohol is usually popular. The person cooking should drink only a very small amount of alcohol, as a drunken cook can be a dangerous one. Watch out for other adults who have been drinking and want to cook.

Remember to keep small children away from the barbecue and warn them about sharp knives and skewers.

Even if a shower of rain interrupts your barbecue, the party can continue – to keep cooking, just pull the lid over the barbecue and open its air vents. Alternatively, take the prepared food inside and carry on cooking under the grill in your kitchen. When the rain stops, the party can move back into the garden!

basic recipes

marinades

Not only do marinades tenderize and flavour ingredients, but they can be brushed on the food as it is cooking to keep it moist and succulent. As a rule, the longer you can leave food to marinate, the better – overnight in the refrigerator is usually ideal. The exception is citrus marinades with fish, as lemon, lime or orange juice begins to 'cook' the fish after about 1 hour.

Mix the marinade and pour it over the ingredients in a shallow, non-metallic dish. Turn the ingredients in the marinade to ensure that they are evenly coated, then cover with clingfilm. Leave the dish in a cool place, rather than the refrigerator, if you are marinating for a short time – up to 1 hour.

Drain the food before cooking, even if you intend to brush it with the marinade. Otherwise, the marinade will drip on the hot coals and may cause them to flare up dangerously. Allow the food to come to room temperature before cooking. If you plan to serve leftover marinade as a sauce with the cooked food, bring it to the boil first to prevent bacterial infection. Better still, reserve some of the mixture in advance so that it never comes into contact with raw meat, poultry or fish.

Allow about 150 ml/5 fl oz marinade to every 450 g/1 lb of food.

red wine marinade

150 ml/5 fl oz red wine
1 tbsp olive oil
1 tbsp red wine vinegar
1 tbsp wholegrain mustard
2 bay leaves, torn or crumbled
2 garlic cloves, finely chopped
pepper

yogurt marinade

4 tbsp natural yogurt
1 tbsp olive oil
1 tbsp balsamic vinegar
1 tbsp Dijon mustard
8 fresh sage leaves, finely chopped
ground white pepper

hot pepper marinade

5 tbsp tomato purée
4 tbsp lime juice
1 tbsp red wine vinegar
2 tsp clear honey
1 tsp Tabasco sauce
1 tsp ground mixed spice
pepper

white wine marinade

150 ml/5 fl oz dry white wine
4 tbsp olive oil
1 tbsp lemon juice
3 tbsp finely chopped fresh parsley
1 garlic clove, finely chopped
pepper

sauces and dressings

Many sauces can be made in advance and they are a simple way to turn a plain chop, burger or drumstick into something special.

mild mustard sauce

2 egg yolks
2 tbsp lemon juice
2 garlic cloves, chopped
300 ml/10 fl oz olive oil
1 tbsp Dijon mustard
salt and pepper

1 Place the egg yolks, lemon juice and garlic in a food processor and process until blended and smooth. With the motor still running, gradually add the olive oil through the feeder tube until thick and creamy.

2 Transfer to a bowl, stir in the mustard and season to taste with salt and pepper.

guacamole

2 avocados
3 spring onions, finely chopped
1 garlic clove, finely chopped
2 fresh green chillies, deseeded and finely chopped
2 tbsp olive oil

4 tbsp lime juice
salt
chopped fresh coriander, to garnish

1 Halve and stone the avocados, then scoop the flesh into a bowl. Roughly mash the avocado flesh with a fork, then stir in the spring onions, garlic, chillies, olive oil and lime juice. Season to taste with salt and sprinkle the chopped coriander on top.

mayonnaise

150 ml/5 fl oz sunflower oil
150 ml/5 fl oz olive oil
2 egg yolks
salt and pepper
1 tbsp white wine vinegar
2 tsp Dijon mustard

1 Mix the oils together in a jug. Beat the egg yolks with a pinch of salt. Gradually add the oil, a drop at a time, beating constantly with a whisk or electric mixer. When one-quarter of the oil has been incorporated, beat in the vinegar. Continue adding the oil, in a steady stream, beating constantly until it is all incorporated and the mixture is thick and creamy. Stir in the mustard and season to taste with salt and pepper.

> **variation**
>
> To make lemon mayonnaise, substitute lemon juice for the white wine vinegar and 1 tablespoon of chopped fresh lemon thyme for the mustard.

fish & seafood

Barbecuing fish gives it a uniquely delicious flavour, but it can be quite tricky to do well, as the fierce heat of the coals can dry out the delicate flesh of even oily fish. This chapter is packed with clever ideas for protecting the texture and simultaneously enhancing the flavour of a wide variety of fish and seafood.

Wrapping fish in a foil parcel, as in Cod & Tomato Parcels (see page 24) is a popular way to barbecue it, keeping it moist and sealing in the flavour. However, there are lots of other, more interesting kinds of wraps, too, from Bacon-wrapped Trout (see page 28) to Mackerel in a Lettuce Jacket (see page 34) and Thai-style banana leaves for Baked Red Mullet (see page 32). Marinades, ranging from refreshing combinations of citrus juice and herbs to fiery mixtures of chilli and spices, not only add flavour, but can be brushed on the fish while it is cooking to ensure succulent results.

The recipes have been inspired by dishes from around the world and there is sure to be something to suit all tastes and appetites, from Japanese Salmon Teriyaki (see page 19) to Australian Surf & Turf Kebabs (see page 48) and from Caribbean Sea Bass (see page 20) to Greek Red Mullet Parcels (see page 33). There are steaks and fillets, whole fish, kebabs, prawns, scallops and even oysters. Recipes include inexpensive fish dishes for family lunches, luxurious centrepieces for special occasion barbecues, simple grills for speed and ease and fabulous sauces and salsas to impress your guests.

caribbean fish kebabs

serves 6   **prep: 10 mins, plus 1 hr marinating**   **cook: 8–10 mins**

Lightly spiced and marinated, these colourful kebabs look and taste delicious. You can use any firm-textured fish, but for an authentic Caribbean flavour, swordfish is perfect.

INGREDIENTS

1 kg/2 lb 4 oz swordfish steaks

3 tbsp olive oil

3 tbsp lime juice

1 garlic clove, finely chopped

1 tsp paprika

salt and pepper

3 onions, cut into wedges

6 tomatoes, cut into wedges

NUTRITIONAL INFORMATION

Calories 274

Protein 32g

Carbohydrate 9g

Sugars 7g

Fat 13g

Saturates 2g

variation

Instead of serving the kebabs with traditional baked potatoes, serve them with baked sweet potatoes.

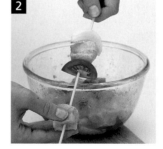

cook's tip

When using wooden skewers, remember to soak them in a bowl of cold water for 30 minutes, as this prevents them burning during cooking.

1 Using a sharp knife, cut the fish into 2.5-cm/ 1-inch cubes and place in a shallow, non-metallic dish. Place the oil, lime juice, garlic and paprika in a jug and mix well. Season to taste with salt and pepper. Pour the marinade over the fish, turning to coat. Cover with clingfilm and leave to marinate in the refrigerator for 1 hour.

2 Preheat the barbecue. Thread the fish cubes, onion wedges and tomato wedges alternately on to 6 long, presoaked wooden skewers. Reserve the marinade.

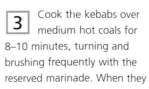

3 Cook the kebabs over medium hot coals for 8–10 minutes, turning and brushing frequently with the reserved marinade. When they are cooked through, transfer the kebabs to a large serving plate and serve immediately.

salmon with mango salsa

serves 4

prep: 15 mins, plus 10 mins standing

cook: 6–8 mins

Although an oily fish, salmon can dry out easily on the fierce heat of the barbecue. Make sure that it is well coated with the citrus juice before you begin cooking.

INGREDIENTS

4 salmon steaks, about 175 g/6 oz each

finely grated rind and juice
of 1 lime or ½ lemon

salt and pepper

SALSA

1 large mango, peeled,
stoned and diced

1 red onion, finely chopped

2 passion fruit

2 fresh basil sprigs

2 tbsp lime juice

salt

NUTRITIONAL INFORMATION

Calories	.360
Protein	.37g
Carbohydrate	.11g
Sugars	.9g
Fat	.20g
Saturates	.3g

1 Preheat the barbecue. Rinse the salmon steaks under cold running water, pat dry with kitchen paper and place in a large, shallow, non-metallic dish. Sprinkle with the lime rind and pour the juice over them. Season to taste with salt and pepper, cover and leave to stand while you make the salsa.

2 Place the mango flesh in a bowl with the onion. Cut the passion fruit in half and scoop out the seeds and pulp with a teaspoon into the bowl. Tear the basil leaves and add them to the bowl with the lime juice. Season to taste with salt and stir well. Cover with clingfilm and reserve until required.

3 Cook the salmon steaks over medium hot coals for 3–4 minutes on each side. Serve immediately with the salsa.

cook's tip

The quickest way to dice the mango is to cut it away from the stone in two halves, slice the flesh in a lattice pattern without cutting through the skin, then turn it inside out and cut away the cubes.

salmon teriyaki

 cook: 10 mins   prep: 10 mins, plus
2 hrs marinating   serves 4

This sweet but piquant Japanese-style teriyaki sauce complements the richness of salmon superbly. Choose some really crisp salad leaves, such as cos or iceberg, to serve with the warm sauce.

NUTRITIONAL INFORMATION	
Calories	.426
Protein	.34g
Carbohydrate	.22g
Sugars	.10g
Fat	.21g
Saturates	.4g

INGREDIENTS

4 salmon fillets, about 175 g/6 oz each

SAUCE

1 tbsp cornflour

125 ml/4 fl oz dark soy sauce

4 tbsp mirin or medium-dry sherry

2 tbsp rice or cider vinegar

2 tbsp clear honey

TO SERVE

½ cucumber

mixed salad leaves, torn into pieces

4 spring onions, thinly sliced diagonally

variation

Replace the salmon with 4 x 115 g/4 oz chicken breast portions. Cut slashes in the meat before marinating and cook for about 15 minutes.

1 Rinse the salmon fillets under cold running water, pat dry with kitchen paper and place in a large, shallow, non-metallic dish. To make the sauce, mix the cornflour and soy sauce together in a jug until a smooth paste forms, then stir in the remaining ingredients. Pour three-quarters of the sauce over the salmon, turning to coat. Cover with clingfilm and leave to marinate in the refrigerator for 2 hours.

2 Preheat the barbecue. Cut the cucumber into batons, then arrange the salad leaves, cucumber and spring onions on 4 serving plates. Pour the remaining sauce into a saucepan and set over the barbecue to warm through.

3 Remove the salmon fillets from the dish and reserve the marinade. Cook the salmon over medium hot coals, brushing frequently with the reserved marinade, for 3–4 minutes on each side. Transfer the salmon fillets to the prepared serving plates and pour the warmed sauce over them. Serve immediately.

caribbean sea bass

cook: 20 mins   **prep: 15 mins**   **serves 6**

NUTRITIONAL INFORMATION

Calories	.211
Protein	.36g
Carbohydrate	.0g
Sugars	.0g
Fat	.7g
Saturates	.1g

variation

Substitute grapefruit and orange slices for the lemon and lime slices in the fish cavity and use oranges wedges to garnish.

This is a magnificent dish to form the centrepiece of a special occasion barbecue and is surprisingly easy to prepare. A fish basket is essential, as it is almost impossible to turn the fish without breaking it up and spoiling its spectacular appearance.

INGREDIENTS

1.5-kg/3 lb 5-oz sea bass, cleaned and scaled	salt and pepper
1–2 tsp olive oil	½ lemon, sliced, plus extra to garnish
1 tsp saffron powder	1 lime, sliced, plus extra to garnish
	1 bunch of fresh thyme

cook's tip

You can scatter a few sprigs of dried thyme over the hot coals while you are cooking the fish for extra aroma. Add them towards the end of cooking as they burn very quickly.

1 Preheat the barbecue. Rinse the sea bass inside and out under cold running water, then pat dry with kitchen paper. Using a sharp knife, make a series of shallow diagonal slashes along each side of the fish. Brush each slash with a little olive oil, then sprinkle over the saffron powder.

2 Brush a large fish basket with olive oil and place the fish in the basket, but do not close it. Season the cavity with salt and pepper. Place the lemon and lime slices and the thyme in the cavity without overfilling it.

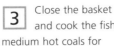

3 Close the basket and cook the fish over medium hot coals for

10 minutes on each side. Carefully transfer to a large serving plate, garnish with lemon and lime slices and serve immediately.

stuffed sardines

serves 6 **prep: 20 mins, plus 1 hr marinating** **cook: 6–8 mins**

Barbecued fresh sardines are always a popular choice. They are usually just plainly grilled, but here they are stuffed with herbs and coated in a mild spice mixture.

INGREDIENTS

15 g/½ oz fresh parsley, finely chopped

4 garlic cloves, finely chopped

12 fresh sardines, cleaned and scaled

3 tbsp lemon juice

85 g/3 oz plain flour

1 tsp ground cumin

salt and pepper

olive oil, for brushing

NUTRITIONAL INFORMATION

Calories 327

Protein 36g

Carbohydrate 12g

Sugars 1g

Fat 16g

Saturates 5g

variation

If you like, substitute the chopped fresh parsley with the same amount of chopped fresh dill or thyme.

cook's tip

To gut sardines, slit open the belly and remove the insides. Rinse the cavity and pat dry. To scale, hold the fish by the tail under cold running water and run your other hand along the body from tail to head.

1 Place the parsley and garlic in a bowl and mix together. Rinse the fish inside and out under cold running water and pat dry with kitchen paper. Spoon the herb mixture into the fish cavities and pat the remainder all over the outside of the fish. Sprinkle the sardines with lemon juice and transfer to a large, shallow, non-metallic dish.

Cover with clingfilm and leave to marinate in the refrigerator for 1 hour.

2 Preheat the barbecue. Mix the flour and ground cumin together in a bowl, then season to taste with salt and pepper. Spread out the seasoned flour on a large plate and gently roll the sardines in the flour to coat.

3 Brush the sardines with olive oil and cook over medium hot coals for 3–4 minutes on each side. Serve immediately.

cod & tomato parcels

cook: 6–10 mins **prep: 10 mins** **serves 4**

variation

Beat 115 g/4 oz softened butter and 2 crushed garlic cloves together, then spread on top of the cod steaks in the parcels and cook as in main recipe.

Cooking cod steaks in this way keeps the flesh deliciously moist and succulent and seals in the flavour of the herbed tomatoes. White wine gives the parcels an added richness.

INGREDIENTS

4 cod steaks, about 175 g/6 oz each

2 tsp extra virgin olive oil

4 tomatoes, peeled and chopped

25 g/1 oz fresh basil leaves, torn into small pieces

4 tbsp white wine

salt and pepper

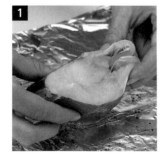

cook's tip

For an attractive presentation, unwrap the parcels and slide the contents, tomato side upwards, on to serving plates. Remove and discard the skin from the outside of the cod steaks before serving.

1 Preheat the barbecue. Rinse the cod steaks under cold running water and pat dry with kitchen paper. Using a sharp knife, cut out and discard the central bones. Cut out 4 rectangles, 33 x 20 cm/13 x 8 inches, from double-thickness foil and brush with the olive oil. Place a cod steak in the centre of each piece of foil.

2 Mix the tomatoes, basil and white wine together in a bowl and season to taste with salt and pepper. Spoon the tomato mixture equally on top of the fish. Bring up the sides of the foil and fold over securely.

3 Cook the cod parcels over hot coals for 3–5 minutes on each side.

Transfer to 4 large serving plates and serve immediately in the parcels.

orange & lemon peppered monkfish

serves 6   **prep: 25 mins, plus 1 hr marinating**   **cook: 20–25 mins**

Although monkfish appears quite expensive, there is very little wastage as, apart from the central backbone, the entire tail is edible. Its flavour is meaty and succulent.

INGREDIENTS

2 oranges

2 lemons

2 monkfish tails, about 500 g/1 lb 2 oz each, skinned and cut into 4 fillets

6 fresh lemon thyme sprigs

2 tbsp olive oil

salt

2 tbsp green peppercorns, lightly crushed

GARNISH

orange wedges

lemon wedges

NUTRITIONAL INFORMATION

Calories 154

Protein 25g

Carbohydrate 5g

Sugars 5g

Fat 4g

Saturates 1g

variation

If you like, you can substitute the green peppercorns with either black, pink or even mixed peppercorns.

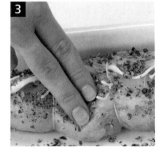

cook's tip

To crush the peppercorns, place them in a polythene bag and, using a rolling pin, lightly crush them. Alternatively, place them in a mortar and crush with a pestle, or grind in a clean coffee mill.

1 Cut 8 orange slices and 8 lemon slices, reserving the remaining fruit. Rinse the monkfish fillets under cold running water and pat dry with kitchen paper. Place 1 fillet from each monkfish tail, cut side up, on a work surface and divide the citrus slices between them. Top with the lemon thyme. Reassemble the tails and tie them securely together at intervals with kitchen string or trussing thread. Place the tails in a large, shallow, non-metallic dish.

2 Squeeze the juice from the remaining fruit and mix with the olive oil in a jug. Season to taste with salt, then spoon the mixture over the fish. Cover with clingfilm and leave to marinate in the refrigerator for up to 1 hour, spooning the marinade over the fish tails once or twice.

3 Preheat the barbecue. Drain the monkfish tails, reserving the marinade. Sprinkle the crushed green peppercorns over the fish, pressing them in with your fingers. Cook the monkfish over medium hot coals, turning and brushing frequently with the reserved marinade, for 20–25 minutes. Transfer to a chopping board, remove and discard the string and cut the monkfish tails into slices. Serve immediately, garnished with orange and lemon wedges.

bacon-wrapped trout

serves 4   **prep: 15 mins** ⏲   **cook: 10–16 mins** ⏲

This classic, pan-fried combination is even more delicious cooked on the barbecue, as the smoky flavour of the bacon becomes more pronounced in contrast to the delicate flesh of the fish.

INGREDIENTS

4 trout, gutted

4 smoked streaky bacon rashers, rinded

4 tbsp plain flour

salt and pepper

2 tbsp olive oil

2 tbsp lemon juice

lamb's lettuce, to serve

GARNISH

fresh parsley sprigs

lemon wedges

NUTRITIONAL INFORMATION

Calories	.448
Protein	.46g
Carbohydrate	.16g
Sugars	.1g
Fat	.23g
Saturates	.6g

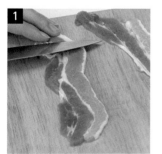

cook's tip

The most commonly available variety of trout is rainbow trout, which is widely farmed. Golden trout, now also farmed, is beginning to appear in most supermarkets and would also work well in this recipe.

1 Preheat the barbecue. Rinse the trout inside and out under cold running water and pat dry with kitchen paper. Stretch the bacon using the back of a heavy, flat-bladed knife.

2 Season the flour with salt and pepper and spread it out on a large, flat plate. Gently roll each trout in the seasoned flour until thoroughly coated. Beginning just below the head, wrap a rasher of bacon in a spiral along the length of each fish.

3 Brush the trout with olive oil and cook over medium hot coals for 5–8 minutes on each side.

Transfer to 4 large serving plates and drizzle with the lemon juice. Garnish with parsley and lemon wedges and serve with lamb's lettuce.

chargrilled tuna with chilli salsa

⏱ **cook: 20 mins**

⏱ **prep: 15 mins, plus 1 hr marinating**

serves 4

A firm fish such as tuna is an excellent choice for barbecues, as it is quite meaty and doesn't break up during cooking. Here it is served with a colourful and spicy chilli salsa.

NUTRITIONAL INFORMATION

Calories 337

Protein 42g

Carbohydrate 5g

Sugars 5g

Fat 16g

Saturates 3g

INGREDIENTS

4 tuna steaks, about 175 g/6 oz each

grated rind and juice of 1 lime

2 tbsp olive oil

salt and pepper

fresh coriander sprigs, to garnish

CHILLI SALSA

2 orange peppers

1 tbsp olive oil

juice of 1 lime

juice of 1 orange

2–3 fresh red chillies, deseeded and chopped

pinch of cayenne pepper

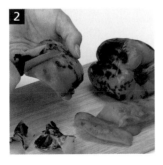

cook's tip

You can make the chilli salsa in advance. Cook the peppers, skin-side upwards, under a preheated hot grill until blackened and charred, then continue as in Step 2.

1 Rinse the tuna thoroughly under cold running water and pat dry with kitchen paper, then place in a large, shallow, non-metallic dish. Sprinkle the lime rind and juice and the olive oil over the fish. Season to taste with salt and pepper, cover with clingfilm and leave to marinate in the refrigerator for up to 1 hour.

2 Preheat the barbecue. To make the salsa, brush the peppers with the olive oil and cook over hot coals, turning frequently, for 10 minutes, or until the skin is blackened and charred. Remove from the barbecue and leave to cool slightly, then peel off the skins and discard the seeds. Put the peppers into a food processor with the remaining salsa ingredients and process to a purée. Transfer to a bowl and season to taste with salt and pepper.

3 Cook the tuna over hot coals for 4–5 minutes on each side, until golden. Transfer to serving plates, garnish with coriander sprigs and serve with the salsa.

mexican tuna

serves 4 **prep: 15 mins, plus 1 hr 30 mins cooling/marinating** **cook: 55 mins**

This spicy, Mexican-style tuna is sure to be a favourite with your adult guests. The mouthwatering, hot flavours of cayenne, chilli and paprika are given an added twist with a dash of tequila.

INGREDIENTS

4 tuna steaks, about 175 g/6 oz each
fresh coriander sprigs, to garnish
lime wedges, to serve

SAUCE
2 tbsp corn oil
2 shallots, finely chopped
1 garlic clove, finely chopped
1 red pepper, deseeded and chopped

2 beef tomatoes, chopped
3 tbsp tomato ketchup
2 tbsp mild mustard
2 tbsp muscovado sugar
1 tbsp clear Mexican honey
1 tbsp cayenne pepper
1 tbsp chilli powder
1 tbsp paprika
1 tbsp tequila

NUTRITIONAL INFORMATION

Calories 410

Protein 44g

Carbohydrate 25g

Sugars 24g

Fat 15g

Saturates 3g

variation

This recipe also works well with other oily fish, such as sea trout or salmon. Replace the lime wedges with lemon, if you prefer.

cook's tip

Fresh tuna is meaty and delicious, and is available all year round. Make sure you choose fresh steaks by looking for firm flesh with a bright reddish-pink colour.

1 To make the sauce, heat the oil in a heavy-based saucepan. Add the shallots and garlic, and cook over a low heat, stirring occasionally, for 5 minutes, or until softened, but not coloured. Add the red pepper and cook for 1 minute, then add the tomatoes and simmer, stirring occasionally, for 20 minutes. Stir in the tomato ketchup, mustard, sugar, honey, cayenne, chilli powder, paprika and tequila and simmer for 20 minutes. Remove the saucepan from the heat and leave to cool.

2 Spoon the sauce into a food processor and process to a smooth purée. Rinse the fish under cold running water and pat dry with kitchen paper. Brush both sides of the tuna fillets with the sauce, place in a shallow dish, cover with clingfilm and leave to marinate in the refrigerator for 1 hour. Reserve the remaining sauce.

3 Preheat the barbecue. Brush the tuna steaks with the sauce and cook over medium hot coals, brushing frequently with the sauce, for 3 minutes on each side. Transfer to serving plates, garnish with fresh coriander sprigs and serve immediately with lime wedges.

baked red mullet

serves 4   **prep: 25 mins**   **cook: 15–20 mins**

Banana leaves are the authentic wrapping used in this Indonesian dish. They are available in Chinese supermarkets – if you buy them frozen, thaw them before use. Alternatively, wrap the fish in foil.

INGREDIENTS

4 banana leaves

2 limes

3 garlic cloves

4 red mullet, about 350 g/12 oz each

2 spring onions, thinly sliced

2.5-cm/1-inch piece fresh root ginger

1 onion, finely chopped

4½ tsp groundnut or corn oil

3 tbsp kecap manis or light soy sauce

1 tsp ground coriander

1 tsp ground cumin

¼ tsp ground cloves

¼ tsp ground turmeric

NUTRITIONAL INFORMATION	
Calories	.233
Protein	.32g
Carbohydrate	.3g
Sugars	.1g
Fat	.10g
Saturates	.0g

cook's tip

Kecap manis is a thick, sweet, Indonesian variety of soy sauce and is available in Chinese supermarkets. If you cannot find it, then use light soy sauce instead.

1 Preheat the barbecue. If necessary, cut the banana leaves into 4 x 40-cm/16-inch squares, using a sharp knife or scissors. Thinly slice ½ a lime and 1 garlic clove. Clean and scale the fish, then rinse it inside and out under cold running water. Pat dry with kitchen paper. Using a sharp knife, make a series of deep diagonal slashes on the side of each fish, then insert the lime and garlic slices into the slashes. Place the fish on the banana leaf squares and sprinkle with the spring onions.

2 Finely chop the remaining garlic and squeeze the juice from the remaining limes. Finely chop the ginger, then place the garlic in a bowl with the onion, ginger, oil, kecap manis, spices and lime juice and mix to a paste.

3 Spoon the paste into the fish cavities and spread it over the outside. Roll up the parcels and tie securely with string. Cook over medium hot coals, turning occasionally, for 15–20 minutes. Serve.

greek red mullet parcels

cook: 16–20 mins

prep: 20 mins, plus 45 mins marinating

serves 4

Although the fish is wrapped in vine leaves, it is worth using a fish basket to ensure that you can turn it during cooking without damage. The vine leaves keep the fish moist and full of flavour.

NUTRITIONAL INFORMATION

Calories	.364
Protein	.33g
Carbohydrate	.1g
Sugars	.0g
Fat	.26g
Saturates	.3g

INGREDIENTS

4 red mullet, about 350 g/12 oz each, cleaned and scaled

salt and pepper

4 garlic cloves, thinly sliced

4 tbsp finely chopped mixed fresh chervil, oregano and rosemary

6 tbsp extra virgin olive oil, plus extra for brushing

2 tbsp red wine vinegar

16–20 vine leaves in brine, drained and rinsed in boiling water

cook's tip

If using fresh vine leaves, trim off the stems, place in a saucepan and add enough cold water to cover. Bring to the boil, then drain immediately and refresh under cold running water.

1 Rinse the fish inside and out under cold running water and pat dry with kitchen paper. Using a sharp knife, make a series of diagonal slashes along each side of the fish. Season the slashes with salt and pepper and fill with the garlic and herbs. Transfer the fish to a large, shallow, non-metallic dish. Mix the oil and vinegar together in a jug and season to taste with salt and pepper. Pour the marinade over the fish, then cover with clingfilm and leave to marinate in the refrigerator for up to 45 minutes.

2 Preheat the barbecue. Brush a fish basket with olive oil. Wrap the fish in the prepared vine leaves, making sure that the entire body is covered. Transfer the fish to the fish basket.

3 Cook the fish over medium hot coals for 8–10 minutes on each side. Serve immediately.

mackerel in a lettuce jacket

⏲ **cook: 35 mins**   ⏱ **prep: 30 mins**   **serves 6**

NUTRITIONAL INFORMATION

Calories 582

Protein 45g

Carbohydrate 14g

Sugars 5g

Fat 39g

Saturates 9g

variation

If you like, replace the gooseberries with the same quantity of roughly chopped rhubarb.

Mackerel has firm-textured flesh with a good flavour. It is very nutritious and makes a filling meal. It is traditionally served with a sharp-tasting sauce, often made with gooseberries, but in this case, they are used as a stuffing. Serve with new potatoes and salad.

INGREDIENTS

24–30 large cos or iceberg lettuce leaves

6 mackerel, cleaned

salt and pepper

2 tbsp creamed horseradish

10 fresh dill sprigs

STUFFING

125 ml/4 fl oz water

2 tbsp lemon juice

1 cooking apple

15 g/½ oz butter

2 shallots, finely chopped

125 g/4½ oz gooseberries, topped and tailed

25 g/1 oz fresh white breadcrumbs

55 g/2 oz medium oatmeal

1 tbsp dry cider

2 tbsp chopped fresh dill

salt and pepper

cook's tip

Cook the parcels seam-side down first to seal for 5 minutes, then carefully turn the parcels over with tongs or a fish slice and cook for a further 5 minutes, or until the fish is tender.

1 Preheat the barbecue. To make the stuffing, pour the water into a bowl and stir in the lemon juice. Peel, core and dice the apple and place in the water. Melt the butter in a saucepan. Add the shallots and cook, stirring occasionally, for 5 minutes, or until softened. Drain the apple, reserving the soaking water, and add to the saucepan with the gooseberries. Cook, stirring, for 2–3 minutes, then add the soaking water. Simmer gently for 5 minutes, until the fruit is tender. Remove from the heat and leave to cool.

2 Meanwhile, blanch the lettuce leaves in boiling water for 10 seconds, then drain and refresh under cold running water.

3 Mix the breadcrumbs, 2 tablespoons of the oatmeal and the cider in a bowl, then stir into the cooled fruit mixture. Stir in the chopped dill and season to taste with salt and pepper. Rinse the mackerel inside and out under cold running water and pat dry. Season the cavities with salt and pepper and spoon in the stuffing.

4 Spread 1 teaspoon of horseradish over the fish and coat with the remaining oatmeal. Arrange 4–5 lettuce leaves to form a rectangle and place 3 dill sprigs in the centre. Top with a fish and wrap the leaves around to enclose all but the head and tail. Repeat with the other fish. Cook over medium hot coals for 10 minutes on each side. Serve.

mixed seafood brochettes

serves 6　　　　**prep: 15 mins, plus 1 hr marinating**　　　　**cook: 20 mins**

Seafood brochettes always look attractive and are perennially popular. Here they are served with a flavoursome sauce for dipping.

INGREDIENTS

2 tbsp sesame seeds	salt and pepper
500 g/1 lb 2 oz swordfish steaks or monkfish fillet	1½ tsp cornflour
	2 tbsp water
350 ml/12 fl oz dry white wine	2 tbsp chopped fresh coriander
2 tbsp corn or sunflower oil	12 prepared scallops
grated rind and juice of 2 limes	12 raw tiger prawns
2 garlic cloves, finely chopped	

variation

For a budget dish, replace half the prawns with tomato wedges and half the scallops with onion wedges. Brush with the marinade during cooking.

cook's tip

Don't peel the prawns as they look more attractive cooked in their shells. Keep an empty bowl handy for the discarded prawns' heads and shells.

1 Dry-fry the sesame seeds in a covered heavy-based frying pan until they begin to pop and give off their aroma. Remove from the heat and reserve. Cut the fish into 2.5-cm/1-inch cubes, then place in a shallow, non-metallic dish. Mix 200 ml/ 7 fl oz of the wine, the oil, lime rind and juice and garlic together in a jug and season to taste with salt and pepper. Pour half of this over the fish, turning to coat, and pour the remainder into a small saucepan. Cover the fish with clingfilm and leave to marinate in a cool place or the refrigerator for up to 1 hour.

2 Preheat the barbecue. Set the saucepan over a low heat and add the remaining wine. Mix the cornflour and water into a smooth paste and stir it into the saucepan, then bring to the boil, stirring constantly, and simmer until thickened. Remove the saucepan from the heat and stir in the coriander and roasted sesame seeds. Cover with a lid and place by the side of the barbecue to keep warm.

3 Remove the fish from the marinade and thread on to 6 metal skewers, alternating with the scallops and prawns. Cook the brochettes over medium hot coals, turning occasionally, for 5–8 minutes, or until the fish is cooked and the prawns have changed colour. Transfer to a large serving plate and serve immediately with the sauce.

indonesian spiced fish

⏲ **cook: 16 mins**　　　　⏲ **prep: 15 mins, plus**　　　　**serves 6**
　　　　　　　　　　　　　1 hr marinating

This exotic barbecued treat looks spectacular and has a flavour to match. Chilli, fresh ginger and lime juice are combined in a spicy paste to coat the fish and permeate its flesh before grilling.

INGREDIENTS

1 kg/2 lb 4 oz sea bream or red snapper

4 garlic cloves, finely chopped

2 fresh red chillies, deseeded and finely chopped

2.5-cm/1-inch piece fresh root ginger, thinly sliced

4 spring onions, chopped

juice of 1 lime

2 tbsp corn oil, plus extra for brushing

salt

shredded coconut, to garnish (optional)

variation

If you like, substitute the corn oil with the same quantity of sunflower oil. You can also replace the lime juice with lemon juice.

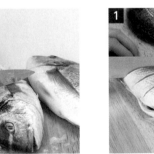

cook's tip

To clean the fish, use a sharp knife to slit open the belly and remove the innards. When scaling fish, it is best to do it either outside or in a polythene bag as the scales can go everywhere.

1 Clean the fish (see cook's tip), then remove the scales, beginning at the tail and working towards the head. Rinse the fish inside and out under cold running water and pat dry with kitchen paper. Using a sharp knife, make a series of diagonal slashes on both sides of the fish. Place it in a large, shallow, non-metallic dish.

2 Put the garlic, chillies, ginger and spring onions into a food processor and process to a paste. Transfer to a small bowl, stir in the lime juice and oil and season to taste with salt. Place 1–2 tablespoons of the spice mixture into the cavity of the fish and spoon the remainder over the fish, turning to coat. Cover with clingfilm and leave to marinate in a cool place or the refrigerator for up to 1 hour.

3 Preheat the barbecue. Lightly brush a fish basket with oil and place the fish in it, reserving the marinade. Cook over medium hot coals, basting frequently with the marinade, for 8 minutes on each side, or until the flesh flakes easily. Serve immediately, garnished with coconut if you like.

sizzling scallops

serves 4   **prep: 10 mins, plus 30 mins marinating**   **cook: 8–10 mins**

This is a new and great way to cook scallops on the barbecue. You can also use other shellfish, such as oysters, if you prefer.

INGREDIENTS

1 lemon

6 tbsp olive oil

salt and pepper

12 prepared scallops

115 g/4 oz fresh wholemeal
breadcrumbs

55 g/2 oz butter, melted

lemon wedges, to garnish (optional)

NUTRITIONAL INFORMATION

Calories 432

Protein 26g

Carbohydrate 15g

Sugars 1g

Fat 30g

Saturates 10g

cook's tip

It is not necessary to cut off the orange coral, if there is any, before coating and cooking the scallops. Leave a small space between each scallop to ensure even cooking.

1 Finely grate the lemon rind, then place it in a dish with the olive oil and mix together. Season to taste. Add the scallops, tossing to coat, then cover and leave to marinate for 30 minutes.

2 Place the breadcrumbs in a large bowl. Add the scallops, one at a time, and toss until they are well coated, then thread on to individual presoaked wooden skewers. Drizzle with the melted butter.

3 Cook the scallops over medium hot coals, turning once, for 8–10 minutes. Transfer to a large serving dish, garnish with lemon wedges, if you like, and serve immediately.

scallops & bacon

⏲ **cook: 10 mins**   ⏱ **prep: 20 mins**   **serves 4**

These scrumptious nibbles are delicious served piping hot with chilled aïoli and a glass of champagne or sparkling wine.

NUTRITIONAL INFORMATION	
Calories	.974
Protein	.55g
Carbohydrate	.5g
Sugars	.0g
Fat	.82g
Saturates	.21g

INGREDIENTS

20 prepared scallops

4 tbsp lemon juice

salt and pepper

20 streaky bacon rashers, rinded

AIOLI

4 garlic cloves, crushed

salt and pepper

2 egg yolks

225 ml/8 fl oz extra virgin olive oil

1 Preheat the barbecue. To make the aïoli, place the garlic in a bowl, add a pinch of salt and mash with the back of a spoon. Add the egg yolks and beat with an electric whisk for 30 seconds, or until creamy. Beat in the olive oil, one drop at a time. As the mixture begins to thicken, add the oil in a steady stream, beating constantly.

Season to taste with salt and pepper, cover the bowl and leave to chill until required.

2 Sprinkle the scallops with the lemon juice and season to taste with salt and pepper. Stretch the bacon rashers with a heavy, flat-bladed knife, then wrap a rasher around each scallop and secure with cocktail sticks.

3 Cook the scallops over medium hot coals for 5 minutes on each side. Transfer to a large serving plate and serve immediately with the aïoli.

variation

These bacon-wrapped scallops are also tasty served with tartare sauce, instead of the aïoli.

chargrilled devils

cook: 5 mins   **prep: 30 mins**   **serves 4**

variation

You can replace the shallot with a small, finely chopped onion and the fresh parsley with the same amount of snipped fresh chives, if you prefer.

This is a barbecue version of the classic appetizer 'angels on horseback', and goes to prove how sophisticated and elegant alfresco dining can be.

INGREDIENTS

36 fresh oysters

18 streaky bacon rashers, rinded

1 tbsp mild paprika

1 tsp cayenne pepper

SAUCE

1 fresh red chilli, deseeded and finely chopped

1 garlic clove, finely chopped

1 shallot, finely chopped

2 tbsp finely chopped fresh parsley

2 tbsp lemon juice

salt and pepper

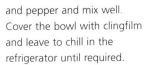

cook's tip

To shuck an oyster, wrap a tea towel around one hand and grasp the oyster, flat shell uppermost. Prise open with a strong knife, then run the blade around the inside of the shell to sever the muscle.

1 Preheat the barbecue. Open the oysters, catching the juice from the shells in a bowl. Cut the oysters from the bottom shells, reserve and tip any remaining juice into the bowl. To make the sauce, add the red chilli, garlic, shallot, parsley and lemon juice to the bowl, then season to taste with salt and pepper and mix well. Cover the bowl with clingfilm and leave to chill in the refrigerator until required.

2 Cut each bacon rasher in half across the centre. Season the oysters with paprika and cayenne, then roll each oyster up inside ½ a bacon rasher. Thread 9 wrapped oysters on to 4 presoaked wooden skewers or cocktail sticks.

3 Cook over hot coals, turning frequently, for 5 minutes, or until the bacon is well browned and crispy. Transfer to a large serving plate and serve immediately with the sauce.

prawns with citrus salsa

serves 6 **prep: 25 mins** ⏲ **cook: 6 mins** ♨

A fruity, herby salsa brings out the flavour of grilled prawns. It can be prepared in advance of the barbecue, then left in the refrigerator to chill until your guests are ready to eat.

INGREDIENTS

36 large, raw tiger prawns

2 tbsp finely chopped fresh coriander

pinch of cayenne pepper

3–4 tbsp corn oil

fresh coriander leaves, to garnish

lime wedges, to serve

SALSA

1 orange

1 tart eating apple, peeled, quartered and cored

2 fresh red chillies, deseeded and chopped

1 garlic clove, chopped

8 fresh coriander sprigs

8 fresh mint sprigs

4 tbsp lime juice

salt and pepper

NUTRITIONAL INFORMATION

Calories 126

Protein 11g

Carbohydrate 5g

Sugars 5g

Fat 7g

Saturates 1g

variation

If you prefer, you can omit the fresh mint from the salsa and add extra coriander instead.

cook's tip

To devein prawns, cut a slit along the back and use the point of the knife to remove the dark intestinal thread. It is not dangerous to eat, but can spoil the flavour.

1 Preheat the barbecue. To make the salsa, peel the orange and cut into segments. Reserve any juice. Put the orange segments, apple quarters, chillies, garlic, coriander and mint into a food processor and process until smooth. With the motor running, add the lime juice through the feeder tube. Transfer the salsa to a serving bowl and season to taste with salt and pepper. Cover with clingfilm and leave to chill in the refrigerator until required.

2 Using a sharp knife, remove and discard the heads from the prawns, then peel off the shells. Cut along the back of the prawns and remove the dark intestinal vein (see cook's tip). Rinse the prawns under cold running water and pat dry with kitchen paper. Mix the chopped coriander, cayenne and corn oil together in a dish. Add the prawns and toss well to coat.

3 Cook the prawns over medium hot coals for 3 minutes on each side, or until they have changed colour. Transfer to a large serving plate, garnish with fresh coriander leaves and serve immediately with lime wedges and the salsa.

coconut prawns

serves 4

prep: 15 mins, plus 1 hr marinating

cook: 8 mins

This classic Thai combination of flavours is perfect with chargrilled prawns, but would also go well with other fish and seafood.

INGREDIENTS

6 spring onions
400 ml/14 fl oz coconut milk
finely grated rind and juice of 1 lime
4 tbsp chopped fresh coriander
2 tbsp corn or sunflower oil
pepper
650 g/1 lb 7 oz raw tiger prawns

GARNISH
lemon wedges
fresh coriander sprigs

NUTRITIONAL INFORMATION

Calories 218

Protein 29g

Carbohydrate 7g

Sugars 6g

Fat 7g

Saturates 1g

cook's tip

Coconut milk is not the same as the liquid from inside the fresh nut. It is available in cans from supermarkets and Chinese food shops.

1 Finely chop the spring onions and place in a large, shallow, non-metallic dish with the coconut milk, lime rind and juice, coriander and oil. Mix well and season to taste with pepper. Add the prawns, turning to coat. Cover with clingfilm and leave to marinate in the refrigerator for 1 hour.

2 Preheat the barbecue. Drain the prawns, reserving the marinade. Thread the prawns on to 8 long metal skewers.

3 Cook the skewers over medium hot coals, brushing with the reserved marinade and turning frequently, for 8 minutes, or until they have changed colour. Cook the lemon wedges, skin-side down over medium hot coals, for the last 5 minutes. Serve the prawns immediately, garnished with the hot lemon wedges and coriander sprigs.

spanish prawns

🕙 **cook: 25 mins**　　　　🕐 **prep: 20 mins**　　　　**serves 6**

These fresh prawns are served with a fiery tomato and chilli sauce.
If you prefer a milder flavour, you can reduce the number of chillies.

NUTRITIONAL INFORMATION	
Calories 175	
Protein 12g	
Carbohydrate 5g	
Sugars 5g	
Fat 12g	
Saturates 2g	

INGREDIENTS

1 bunch of fresh flat-leaved parsley

36 large, raw Mediterranean prawns,
peeled and deveined, tails left on

3–4 tbsp olive oil

lemon wedges, to garnish

SAUCE

6 fresh red chillies

1 onion, chopped

2 garlic cloves, chopped

500 g/1 lb 2 oz tomatoes, chopped

3 tbsp olive oil

pinch of sugar

salt and pepper

cook's tip

To make the prawns easier to turn, thread them individually on to small, presoaked wooden skewers. Spread the skewers out on the grill rack to ensure that they are evenly cooked.

1 Preheat the barbecue. Chop enough parsley to fill 2 tablespoons and reserve. To make the sauce, deseed and chop the chillies, then put into a food processor with the onion and garlic and process until finely chopped. Add the tomatoes and olive oil and process to a purée.

2 Transfer the mixture to a saucepan set over a very low heat, stir in the sugar and season to taste with salt and pepper. Simmer very gently, without boiling, for 15 minutes. Transfer the sauce to an earthenware bowl and place on the side of the barbecue to keep warm.

3 Rinse the prawns under cold running water and pat dry on kitchen paper. Mix the parsley and olive oil in a dish, add the prawns and toss well to coat. Cook the prawns over medium hot coals for 3 minutes on each side, or until they have changed colour. Transfer to a plate, garnish with lemon wedges and serve with the sauce.

surf & turf kebabs

cook: 6–10 mins   **prep: 20 mins**   **serves 4**

NUTRITIONAL INFORMATION

Calories 516

Protein 50g

Carbohydrate 23g

Sugars 18g

Fat 26g

Saturates 5g

variation

Other types of vegetables are also suitable for these kebabs, such as strips of red pepper and baby onions.

An Australian favourite that offers the best of both worlds – prawns from the surf and meat from the turf. The different kebabs are each coated with a flavoured oil before cooking.

INGREDIENTS

12 raw tiger prawns

4 shallots, halved

12 cherry tomatoes

2 tbsp sunflower oil

½ tsp ground coriander

pepper

STEAK KEBABS

400 g/14 oz rump steak, cut into 2.5-cm/1-inch cubes

4 onions, quartered

8 bay leaves

2 tbsp sunflower oil

½–¾ tsp chilli powder

CHICKEN KEBABS

400 g/14 oz skinless, boneless chicken breasts, cut into 2.5-cm/1-inch cubes

2 courgettes, thickly sliced

2 fresh pineapple slices, cut into cubes

2 tbsp sunflower oil

2 tbsp dark soy sauce

2 tbsp redcurrant jelly

pepper

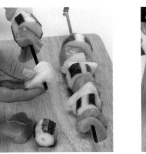

cook's tip

If using metal skewers, brush them with a little oil before threading the pieces of food on to them. This prevents the food sticking to them during cooking.

1 Preheat the barbecue. Remove the heads from the prawns. Thread the shallots, prawns and cherry tomatoes alternately on to 4 metal skewers. Thread the steak, onion quarters and bay leaves alternately on to 4 metal skewers. Thread the chicken, courgette slices and pineapple cubes alternately on to 4 metal skewers.

2 For the prawn kebabs, mix the oil and ground coriander together in a small bowl and season to taste with pepper, then brush all over the kebabs. For the steak kebabs, mix the oil and chilli powder to taste in a separate bowl, then brush all over the kebabs. For the chicken kebabs, mix the oil, soy sauce and redcurrant jelly together in a third bowl and season to taste with pepper, then brush all over the kebabs.

3 Cook the prawn kebabs over medium hot coals, turning frequently and brushing with any remaining coriander-flavoured oil, for 6–8 minutes. Cook the steak kebabs on the hottest part of the barbecue, turning frequently and brushing with any remaining chilli-flavoured oil, for 5–8 minutes. Cook the chicken kebabs over medium hot coals for 6–10 minutes, turning frequently and brushing with any remaining soy-flavoured oil. Serve when the kebabs are all cooked.

poultry

Chicken is one of the most popular barbecue foods and this chapter certainly explores its dazzling versatility. Whether drumsticks, quarters, breast portions, wings or kebabs, the sometimes bland meat is ideal for an immense range of flavourings and marinades. Whether you like it hot and spicy, subtle and aromatic, rich and full-flavoured or fruity and refreshing, you are sure to find a chicken dish to set your taste buds tingling. There are familiar favourites, such as Mustard & Honey Drumsticks (see page 54) and Chicken Tikka (see page 72), as well as some more unusual grills, such as Jamaican Kebabs (see page 56) and Italian Devilled Chicken (see page 70).

Many of the chicken recipes can be easily adapted for cooking turkey breasts and steaks and this chapter also includes some specific turkey grills, such as tasty little Turkey Rolls (see page 77), served with colourful redcurrant relish – a perfect choice for guests. Duck is an excellent meat for cooking on the barbecue because it is naturally quite fatty. This ensures that it stays moist. However, for entertaining guests, there is little that is more impressive than Sage & Lemon Poussins (see page 60) – young chickens that have been spatchcocked and cooked whole.

As well as marinades, many of the recipes include tasty sauces, salsas, pesto and tapenades. Try Drumsticks in a Piquant Dressing (see page 55), Spicy Chicken Wings (see page 68) with a colourful pepper sauce or Spicy Pitta Pockets (see page 74) with a fiery chilli sauce. Mix and match the sauces to suit your family's tastes and to extend your barbecue repertoire.

cajun chicken

cook: 25–30 mins **prep: 10 mins** **serves 4**

NUTRITIONAL INFORMATION

Calories 388

Protein 19g

Carbohydrate 6g

Sugars 1g

Fat 32g

Saturates 15g

variation

Try the spice mix on swordfish steaks. Coat the fish and corn separately, then cook the corn for 15 minutes and the fish for 6–8 minutes.

Chicken and corn are coated in an aromatic mixture before being blackened – slightly charred – on the barbecue to bring out the many flavours of the different spices.

INGREDIENTS

4 chicken drumsticks

4 chicken thighs

2 fresh corn cobs, husks and silks removed

85 g/3 oz butter, melted

1 tsp garlic powder

1 tsp dried thyme

1 tsp cayenne pepper

1 tsp ground black pepper

½ tsp ground white pepper

¼ tsp ground cumin

SPICE MIX

2 tsp onion powder

2 tsp paprika

1½ tsp salt

cook's tip

To remove the husks from the corn cobs, gently pull them away from the corn towards the base, then cut off the base and remove the silk.

1 Preheat the barbecue. Using a sharp knife, make 2–3 diagonal slashes in the chicken drumsticks and thighs, then place them in a large dish. Cut the corn cobs into thick slices and add them to the dish. Mix all the ingredients for the spice mix together in a small bowl.

2 Brush the chicken and corn with the melted butter and sprinkle with the spice mix. Toss to coat well.

3 Cook the chicken over medium hot coals, turning occasionally, for 15 minutes, then add the corn slices and cook, turning occasionally, for a further 10–15 minutes, or until beginning to blacken slightly at the edges. Transfer to a large serving plate and serve immediately.

mustard & honey drumsticks

serves 4   **prep: 10 mins, plus 1 hr marinating**   **cook: 25–30 mins**

Chicken can taste rather bland, but this sweet-and-sour glaze gives it a wonderful piquancy and helps to keep it moist during cooking.

INGREDIENTS

8 chicken drumsticks

fresh parsley sprigs, to garnish

salad, to serve

GLAZE

125 ml/4 fl oz clear honey

4 tbsp Dijon mustard

4 tbsp wholegrain mustard

4 tbsp white wine vinegar

2 tbsp sunflower oil

salt and pepper

NUTRITIONAL INFORMATION	
Calories	.409
Protein	.32g
Carbohydrate	.27g
Sugars	.26g
Fat	.19g
Saturates	.4g

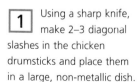

variation

Try this glaze with pork spare ribs. Marinate 900 g/ 2 lb spare ribs in the glaze for 1 hour. Cook over hot coals, turning frequently and brushing with the glaze, for 15–20 minutes.

1 Using a sharp knife, make 2–3 diagonal slashes in the chicken drumsticks and place them in a large, non-metallic dish.

2 Mix all the ingredients for the glaze together in a jug and season to taste with salt and pepper. Pour the glaze over the drumsticks, turning until the drumsticks are well coated. Cover with clingfilm and leave to marinate in the refrigerator for at least 1 hour.

3 Preheat the barbecue. Drain the chicken drumsticks, reserving the marinade. Cook the chicken over medium hot coals, turning frequently and brushing with the reserved marinade, for 25–30 minutes, or until thoroughly cooked. Transfer to serving plates, garnish with fresh parsley sprigs and serve immediately with salad.

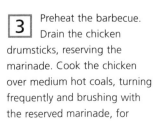

drumsticks in a piquant dressing

🕙 **cook: 2 hrs**

🕒 **prep: 10 mins, plus 20 mins cooling**

serves 6

This tasty dressing gives the chicken drumsticks a rich colour as well as a fabulous flavour, which makes them irresistibly appetizing.

NUTRITIONAL INFORMATION

Calories	.266
Protein	.31g
Carbohydrate	.13g
Sugars	.13g
Fat	.10g
Saturates	.3g

INGREDIENTS

12 chicken drumsticks

DRESSING

1 onion, chopped

1 celery stick, chopped

1 garlic clove, finely chopped

800 g/1 lb 12 oz canned chopped tomatoes

3 tbsp muscovado sugar

1 tbsp paprika

¼ tsp Tabasco sauce

1 tbsp Worcestershire sauce

pepper

cook's tip

There are 2 types of paprika – sweet, which is fairly mild tasting, and hot, which is spicier. However, neither type is as hot as cayenne pepper.

1 Preheat the barbecue. To make the dressing, place all the ingredients in a heavy-based saucepan and bring to the boil over a low heat. Cover and simmer gently for 1 hour, or until the onion and celery are very tender. Remove the saucepan from the heat and leave to cool.

2 Transfer the dressing to a food processor and process to a purée. Using a metal spoon, gently rub the purée through a fine-meshed sieve into a clean saucepan and bring to the boil over a low heat. Simmer gently for 25 minutes, or until reduced and thickened.

3 Brush the drumsticks with the sauce and cook over medium hot coals, turning and brushing with the sauce frequently, for 25–30 minutes. Serve. If you wish to serve the remaining sauce with the drumsticks, make sure that it is returned to boiling point first.

jamaican kebabs

serves 4 **prep: 15 mins, plus 1 hr marinating** **cook: 6-10 mins**

What could be better on a hot summer's day than barbecued chicken kebabs flavoured with tropical fruit and a dash of rum? Serve with a crisp green salad for a filling barbecue lunch.

INGREDIENTS

2 mangoes

4 skinless, boneless chicken breasts, about 175 g/6 oz each, cut into 2.5-cm/1-inch cubes

finely grated rind and juice of 1 lime

1 tbsp dark rum

1 tbsp muscovado sugar

1 tsp ground mixed spice

NUTRITIONAL INFORMATION

Calories 270

Protein 39g

Carbohydrate 15g

Sugars 15g

Fat 6g

Saturates 2g

---

variation

Try substituting diced turkey breast for the chicken, white wine for the rum and cinnamon for the mixed spice.

cook's tip

Make sure that the chicken cubes are all roughly the same size to ensure that they take the same amount of time to cook. Before serving, make sure that they are cooked through.

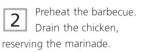

1 Cut the mango into cubes. Using a sharp knife, cut the flesh from either side of the stone in 2 slices and trim off any flesh still clinging to it. Cut through the flesh in a diamond pattern, but do not cut through the skin. Turn the skin inside out and cut away the cubed flesh. Reserve until required. Place the chicken in a shallow,

non-metallic dish. Sprinkle the lime rind and juice over the chicken and add the rum, sugar and mixed spice. Toss the chicken pieces until well coated, cover with clingfilm and leave to marinate in the refrigerator for 1 hour.

2 Preheat the barbecue. Drain the chicken, reserving the marinade.

Thread the chicken pieces and mango cubes alternately on to 8 presoaked wooden skewers.

3 Cook the chicken over medium hot coals, turning and brushing frequently with the marinade, for 6–10 minutes, or until thoroughly cooked. Transfer to a large serving plate and serve immediately.

zesty kebabs

cook: 6–10 mins

prep: 10 mins, plus 8 hrs marinating

serves 4

NUTRITIONAL INFORMATION	
Calories	.290
Protein	.38g
Carbohydrate	.10g
Sugars	.10g
Fat	.11g
Saturates	.3g

These lovely, fresh-tasting chicken kebabs are marinated in a zingy mixture of citrus juice and rind. They are very easy to make and make a perfect main course for a barbecue party.

INGREDIENTS

4 skinless, boneless chicken breasts, about 175 g/6 oz each

finely grated rind and juice of ½ lemon

finely grated rind and juice of ½ orange

2 tbsp clear honey

2 tbsp olive oil

2 tbsp chopped fresh mint

¼ tsp ground coriander

salt and pepper

GARNISH

fresh mint sprigs

citrus zest

variation

Substitute the lemon rind with the same quantity of lime rind and replace the chopped fresh mint with the same quantity of coriander or parsley.

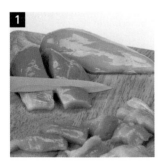

cook's tip

Don't squash the chicken cubes too tightly together on the skewers, otherwise they will not cook evenly and the centres will not properly cook through.

1 Using a sharp knife, cut the chicken into 2.5-cm/1-inch cubes, then place them in a large glass bowl. Place the lemon and orange rind, the lemon and orange juice, the honey, oil, mint and ground coriander in a jug and mix together. Season to taste with salt and pepper. Pour the marinade over the chicken cubes and toss until they are thoroughly coated. Cover with clingfilm and leave to marinate in the refrigerator for up to 8 hours.

2 Preheat the barbecue. Drain the chicken cubes, reserving the marinade. Thread the chicken on to several long metal skewers.

3 Cook the skewers over medium hot coals, turning and brushing frequently with the reserved marinade, for 6–10 minutes, or until thoroughly cooked. Transfer to a large serving plate, garnish with fresh mint sprigs and citrus zest and serve immediately.

sage & lemon poussins

serves 4 **prep: 30 mins** **cook: 20–30 mins**

Spatchcocked poussins are the ideal choice for a barbecue, as they are easy to handle and look attractive. You can buy them ready prepared or spatchcock them yourself.

INGREDIENTS

4 poussins, about 450 g/1 lb each

1 lemon

2 tbsp chopped fresh sage

salt and pepper

GARNISH

fresh herb sprigs

lemon slices

NUTRITIONAL INFORMATION	
Calories 375	
Protein 39g	
Carbohydrate 0g	
Sugars 0g	
Fat 24g	
Saturates 7g	

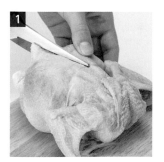

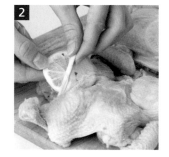

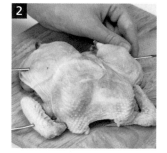

cook's tip

You can thread the skewers crossways through the poussin. Push a skewer through a wing and out through the thigh on the opposite side. Repeat with the other skewer on the other side.

1 Preheat the barbecue. To spatchcock the poussins, turn 1 bird breast-side down and, using strong kitchen scissors or poultry shears, cut through the skin and ribcage along both sides of the backbone, from tail to neck. Remove the backbone and turn the bird breast-side up. Press down firmly on the breastbone with the heel of your hand to flatten. Fold the wingtips underneath. Repeat with the remaining poussins.

2 Thinly slice half the lemon and finely grate the rind of the other half. Mix the lemon rind and sage together in a small bowl. Loosen the skin on the breasts and legs of the poussins and insert the lemon and sage mixture. Tuck in the lemon slices and smooth the skin back firmly. Push a metal skewer through one wing, the top of the breast and out of the other wing. Push a second skewer through one thigh, the bottom of the breast and out the other thigh. Season to taste with salt and pepper.

3 Cook the poussins over medium hot coals for 10–15 minutes on each side. Serve immediately, garnished with fresh herb sprigs and lemon slices.

jerk chicken

cook: 30–35 mins

prep: 15 mins, plus 8 hrs marinating

serves 4

Jerk seasoning – a mixture of herbs and spices – is a Jamaican flavouring that was originally used only for pork. It is equally delicious with chicken and this dish is now extremely popular.

NUTRITIONAL INFORMATION

Calories	.258
Protein	.38g
Carbohydrate	.4g
Sugars	.3g
Fat	.10g
Saturates	.2g

INGREDIENTS

2 fresh red chillies

2 tbsp corn oil, plus extra for brushing

2 garlic cloves, finely chopped

1 tbsp finely chopped onion

1 tbsp finely chopped spring onion

1 tbsp white wine vinegar

1 tbsp lime juice

2 tsp demerara sugar

1 tsp dried thyme

1 tsp ground cinnamon

1 tsp ground mixed spice

¼ tsp freshly grated nutmeg

salt and pepper

4 chicken quarters

cook's tip

For a side dish, trim 2 plantains, cook in a saucepan of boiling water for 20 minutes, drain and cool. Peel, cut into thin 5-cm/2-inch pieces, fold in half and thread on to skewers. Oil and cook for 6 minutes.

1 Deseed and finely chop the red chillies, then place them in a small glass bowl with the oil, garlic, onion, spring onion, vinegar, lime juice, sugar, thyme, cinnamon, mixed spice and nutmeg. Season to taste with salt and pepper and mash thoroughly with a fork.

2 Using a sharp knife, make a series of diagonal slashes in the chicken pieces and place them in a large, shallow, non-metallic dish. Spoon the jerk seasoning over the chicken, rubbing it well into the slashes. Cover and leave to marinate in the refrigerator for up to 8 hours.

3 Preheat the barbecue. Remove the chicken from the marinade, discarding the marinade, brush with oil and cook over medium hot coals, turning frequently, for 30–35 minutes. Transfer to plates and serve.

thai chicken

cook: 30–35 mins

prep: 10 mins, plus 8 hrs marinating

serves 4

NUTRITIONAL INFORMATION

Calories 268

Protein 33g

Carbohydrate 9g

Sugars 6g

Fat 11g

Saturates 3g

variation

To make a sauce, mix 4 tablespoons fish sauce, 2 tablespoons lemon juice, 2 crushed garlic cloves, 1 tablespoon sugar and 1 tablespoon chilli powder.

Roadside stalls serve meals and snacks throughout the day and night in every Thai city. Spicy barbecued chicken is the number one favourite. Serve with a green salad for a delicious barbecue lunch.

INGREDIENTS

4 chicken quarters or 8 chicken pieces

2 lemon grass stalks, roughly chopped

6 garlic cloves, roughly chopped

1 bunch spring onions, roughly chopped

2.5-cm/1-inch piece fresh root ginger, roughly chopped

½ bunch coriander roots, roughly chopped

1 tbsp palm sugar

125 ml/4 fl oz coconut milk

2 tbsp Thai fish sauce (nam pla)

2 tbsp dark soy sauce

lime wedges, to garnish

cook's tip

Palm sugar, coriander roots, coconut milk and Thai fish sauce are all available from specialist Chinese foodshops. If you cannot find palm sugar, then use brown sugar instead.

1 Place the chicken in a single layer in a large, shallow, non-metallic dish. Put the lemon grass, garlic, spring onions, ginger, coriander roots, sugar, coconut milk, fish sauce and soy sauce into a food processor and process to a smooth purée. Pour the spice mixture over the chicken, turning until the chicken is thoroughly coated. Cover the dish with clingfilm and leave to marinate in the refrigerator for up to 8 hours.

2 Preheat the barbecue. Drain the chicken, reserving the marinade.

3 Cook over medium hot coals, turning and brushing frequently with the reserved marinade, for 30–35 minutes, or until thoroughly cooked. Serve immediately, garnished with lime wedges.

hot red chicken

⏱ **cook: 25–30 mins** ⏱ **prep: 10 mins, plus 8 hrs marinating** **serves 4**

NUTRITIONAL INFORMATION

Calories	243
Protein	. . . . .39g
Carbohydrate	. . . . .3g
Sugars	. . . . .3g
Fat	. . . . .8g
Saturates	. . . . .2g

variation

You can also serve this dish with garlic naan bread or plenty of crusty bread or even freshly cooked rice.

In this adaptation of a traditional Indian recipe for spring chickens, chicken pieces are used, but you could substitute spatchcocked poussins (see page 60) if you prefer.

INGREDIENTS

1 tbsp curry paste

1 tbsp tomato ketchup

1 tsp Indian five-spice powder

1 fresh red chilli, deseeded and finely chopped

1 tsp Worcestershire sauce

1 tsp sugar

salt

8 skinless chicken pieces

vegetable oil, for brushing

naan bread, to serve

GARNISH

lemon wedges

fresh coriander sprigs

cook's tip

All curry pastes tend to be quite fiery, but some are hotter than others. Use with caution until you find a variety that suits your palate.

1 Place the curry paste, tomato ketchup, five-spice powder, chilli, Worcestershire sauce and sugar in a small bowl, and stir until the sugar has dissolved. Season to taste with salt.

2 Place the chicken pieces in a large, shallow, non-metallic dish and spoon the spice paste over them, rubbing it in well. Cover with clingfilm and leave to marinate in the refrigerator for up to 8 hours.

3 Preheat the barbecue. Remove the chicken from the spice paste, discarding any remaining paste, and brush with oil. Cook the chicken over medium hot coals, turning occasionally, for 25–30 minutes. Briefly heat the naan bread on the barbecue and serve with the chicken, garnished with lemon wedges and coriander sprigs.

chicken satay

serves 4 **prep: 20 mins, plus 8 hrs marinating** **cook: 10 mins**

This is a delicious dish to serve at a barbecue. Threading the marinated chicken on to the skewers is a messy business, but the results are worth it.

INGREDIENTS

8 tbsp crunchy peanut butter

1 onion, roughly chopped

1 garlic clove, roughly chopped

2 tbsp creamed coconut

4 tbsp groundnut oil

1 tsp light soy sauce

2 tbsp lime juice

2 fresh red chillies, deseeded and chopped

3 kaffir lime leaves, torn

4 skinless, boneless chicken breasts, about 175 g/6 oz each, cut into 2.5-cm/1-inch cubes

NUTRITIONAL INFORMATION

Calories 656

Protein 52g

Carbohydrate 8g

Sugars 5g

Fat 47g

Saturates 12g

variation

Substitute 450 g/1 lb raw tiger prawns for the chicken and cook for 3–4 minutes on each side.

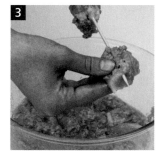

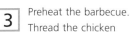

cook's tip

Before cooking the chicken skewers on the lit barbecue, brush the grill rack with a little vegetable or sunflower oil to prevent the meat sticking to it.

1 Put the peanut butter, onion, garlic, coconut, groundnut oil, soy sauce, lime juice, chillies and lime leaves into a food processor and process to a smooth paste. Transfer the paste to a large, glass bowl.

2 Add the chicken cubes to the dish and stir to coat thoroughly. Cover with clingfilm and leave to marinate in the refrigerator for up to 8 hours.

3 Preheat the barbecue. Thread the chicken cubes on to several presoaked wooden skewers, reserving the marinade. Cook the skewers over medium hot coals, turning and brushing frequently with the marinade, for 10 minutes, or until thoroughly cooked. Transfer to a large serving plate and serve immediately.

spicy chicken wings

cook: 18–20 mins

prep: 15 mins, plus 8 hrs marinating

serves 4

NUTRITIONAL INFORMATION

Calories 363

Protein 26g

Carbohydrate 29g

Sugars 27g

Fat 16g

Saturates 3g

variation

Substitute the orange and yellow peppers for red and green ones. Alternatively, just use red peppers.

Coated in a spicy marinade and served with a colourful, chargrilled pepper sauce, these delicious chicken wings are perfect as part of a summer barbecue lunch party.

INGREDIENTS

16 chicken wings

4 tbsp sunflower oil

4 tbsp light soy sauce

5-cm/2-inch piece of fresh root ginger, roughly chopped

2 garlic cloves, roughly chopped

juice and grated rind of 1 lemon

2 tsp ground cinnamon

2 tsp ground turmeric

4 tbsp clear honey

salt and pepper

SAUCE

2 orange peppers

2 yellow peppers

sunflower oil, for brushing

125 ml/4 fl oz natural yogurt

2 tbsp dark soy sauce

2 tbsp chopped fresh coriander

cook's tip

If you prefer, you can snip off the ends of the chicken wings with a pair of strong kitchen scissors to make them look more attractive.

1 Place the chicken wings in a large, shallow, non-metallic dish. Put the oil, soy sauce, ginger, garlic, lemon rind and juice, cinnamon, turmeric and honey into a food processor and process to a smooth purée. Season to taste with salt and pepper. Spoon the mixture over the chicken wings and turn until thoroughly coated, cover with clingfilm and leave to marinate in the refrigerator for up to 8 hours.

2 Preheat the barbecue. To make the sauce, brush the peppers with the oil and cook over hot coals, turning frequently, for 10 minutes, or until the skin is blackened and charred. Remove from the barbecue and leave to cool slightly, then peel off the skins and discard the seeds. Put the flesh into a food processor with the yogurt and process to a smooth purée. Transfer to a bowl and stir in the soy sauce and chopped coriander.

3 Drain the chicken wings, reserving the marinade. Cook over medium hot coals, turning and brushing frequently with the reserved marinade, for 8–10 minutes, or until thoroughly cooked. Serve immediately with the sauce.

italian devilled chicken

serves 4 | prep: 10 mins, plus 8 hrs marinating | cook: 6–10 mins

Peperoncini, the red chillies of the Abruzzi region of Italy, are so hot that they are known as little devils. They are said to be 'as fiery as Lucifer himself'.

INGREDIENTS

4 skinless, boneless chicken breasts, about 175 g/6 oz each, cut into 2.5-cm/1-inch cubes

125 ml/4 fl oz olive oil

finely grated rind and juice of 1 lemon

2 garlic cloves, finely chopped

2 tsp finely chopped dried red chillies

salt and pepper

fresh flat-leaved parsley sprigs, to garnish

NUTRITIONAL INFORMATION

Calories	.403
Protein	.38g
Carbohydrate	.1g
Sugars	.1g
Fat	.28g
Saturates	.5g

variation

You can also make these kebabs with dark chicken meat, such as skinless, boneless thighs.

1 Place the chicken cubes in a large, shallow, non-metallic dish. Place the olive oil, lemon rind and juice, garlic and chillies in a jug and stir together until well blended. Season to taste with salt and pepper.

2 Pour the mixture over the chicken and stir gently to coat. Cover with clingfilm and leave to marinate in the refrigerator for up to 8 hours.

3 Preheat the barbecue. Drain the chicken, reserving the marinade. Thread the chicken on to several presoaked wooden skewers and cook over medium hot coals, turning and brushing frequently with the reserved marinade, for 6–10 minutes, or until thoroughly cooked. Transfer to a large serving dish, garnish with parsley sprigs and serve immediately.

blackened chicken

cook: 6 mins **prep: 10 mins** **serves 4**

Blackened dishes – seasoned and chargrilled – are now virtually synonymous with Cajun cooking, but are not, in fact, traditional and were invented relatively recently.

NUTRITIONAL INFORMATION	
Calories	.229
Protein	.39g
Carbohydrate	.2g
Sugars	.2g
Fat	.7g
Saturates	.2g

INGREDIENTS

4 skinless, boneless whole chicken breasts, about 175 g/6 oz each

2 tbsp natural yogurt

1 tbsp lemon juice

1 garlic clove, very finely chopped

1 tsp paprika

1 tsp ground cumin

1 tsp mustard powder

½ tsp dried thyme

½ tsp dried oregano

½ tsp cayenne pepper

sunflower oil, for brushing

thinly sliced onion rings, to garnish

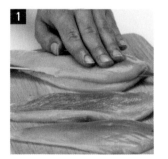

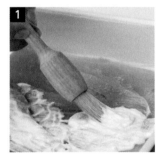

cook's tip

If you like, substitute tuna steaks for the chicken, but don't cut them in half. Cook over medium hot coals for 4 minutes on each side, then serve immediately.

1 Preheat the barbecue. Using a sharp knife, slice the chicken breasts in half horizontally and flatten them slightly with your hand. Place the chicken pieces in a large, shallow, non-metallic dish. Mix the yogurt and lemon juice together in a small bowl and brush the mixture all over the chicken.

2 Mix the garlic, paprika, cumin, mustard powder, thyme, oregano and cayenne together in a separate bowl and sprinkle the mixture evenly over the chicken.

3 Brush the chicken pieces with oil and cook over medium hot coals for 3 minutes on each side, or until beginning to blacken and the chicken is thoroughly cooked. Transfer to a large serving plate and garnish with thinly sliced onion rings. Serve immediately.

chicken tikka

cook: 15 mins

prep: 15 mins, plus 8 hrs marinating

serves 4

This colourful dish looks immensely appetizing and the aroma as it cooks is out of this world – it lives up to its promise, too.

NUTRITIONAL INFORMATION

Calories 228

Protein 33g

Carbohydrate 9g

Sugars 9g

Fat 7g

Saturates 2g

variation

Add colour to a special occasion dish by using red onions instead of the ordinary yellow onions for the garnish.

INGREDIENTS

500 g/1 lb 2 oz skinless, boneless chicken, cut into 5-cm/2-inch cubes

1 garlic clove, finely chopped

1-cm/½-inch piece fresh root ginger, finely chopped

150 ml/5 fl oz natural yogurt

4 tbsp lemon juice

1 tsp chilli powder

¼ tsp ground turmeric

1 tbsp chopped fresh coriander

vegetable oil, for brushing

naan bread, to serve

RAITA

½ cucumber

1 fresh green chilli, deseeded and finely chopped

300 ml/10 fl oz natural yogurt

¼ tsp ground cumin

salt

GARNISH

thinly sliced onion rings

fresh coriander sprigs

lemon wedges

cook's tip

Fresh chillies can burn the skin several hours after chopping, so it is advisable to wear gloves when handling them. Alternatively, wash your hands thoroughly afterwards.

1 Place the chicken in a large glass bowl. Add the garlic, ginger, yogurt, lemon juice, chilli powder, turmeric and coriander and stir well. Cover with clingfilm and leave to marinate in the refrigerator for up to 8 hours.

2 Preheat the barbecue. To make the raita, cut the cucumber into thick slices, then chop finely. Place the cucumber and chilli in a bowl and beat in the yogurt with a fork. Stir in the cumin and season to taste with salt. Cover and leave to chill in the refrigerator until required.

3 Thread the chicken cubes on to presoaked wooden skewers and brush with oil. Cook the chicken over medium hot coals, turning and brushing frequently with oil, for 15 minutes, or until thoroughly cooked. Briefly heat the naan bread on the barbecue. Remove the chicken from the skewers and place on individual serving plates. Garnish with onion rings, coriander sprigs and lemon wedges and serve with the naan bread and the raita.

spicy pitta pockets

serves 4

prep: 30 mins, plus 2 hrs marinating

cook: 35 mins

For convenience, the chicken is cooked on skewers and then combined with salad to fill pitta breads.

INGREDIENTS

500 g/1 lb 2 oz skinless, boneless chicken, cut into 2.5-cm/1-inch cubes

3 tbsp natural yogurt

1 tsp chilli powder

3 tbsp lime juice

1 tbsp chopped fresh coriander

1 fresh green chilli, deseeded and finely chopped

1 tbsp sunflower oil

salt

4 pitta breads

¼ iceberg lettuce, shredded

2 tomatoes, thinly sliced

8 spring onions, chopped

1 tbsp lemon juice

8 bottled jalapeño chillies, drained

SAUCE

2 tbsp sunflower oil

1 onion, chopped

2 garlic cloves, crushed

4 large tomatoes, peeled, deseeded and chopped

2 fresh red chillies, deseeded and chopped

pinch of ground cumin

salt and pepper

variation

If you prefer a milder dish, omit the bottled jalapeño chillies and use 1 fresh red chilli, deseeded and chopped, added to the sauce.

cook's tip

When threading the cubes of chicken on to the skewers, leave a small space between each piece to ensure that the meat cooks evenly.

1 Place the chicken in a large bowl. Mix the yogurt, chilli powder, lime juice, fresh coriander, green chilli and sunflower oil together in a jug and season to taste with salt. Pour the mixture over the chicken and turn until the chicken is coated. Cover with clingfilm and leave to marinate in the refrigerator for 2 hours.

2 Preheat the barbecue. To make the chilli sauce, heat the oil in a small saucepan. Add the onion and garlic and cook over a low heat, stirring occasionally, for 10 minutes, or until softened and golden. Add the tomatoes, chillies and cumin and season to taste with salt and pepper. Simmer gently for 15 minutes, or until reduced and thickened.

3 Set the saucepan of chilli sauce on the side of the barbecue to keep warm. Drain the chicken, reserving the marinade. Thread the chicken on to presoaked wooden skewers. Cook over medium hot coals, turning and brushing frequently with the reserved marinade, for 6–10 minutes, or until thoroughly cooked.

Meanwhile, slit the pitta breads with a sharp knife and toast briefly on the barbecue. Remove the chicken from the skewers and fill the pitta breads with lettuce, tomato slices, spring onions and chicken. Sprinkle with lemon juice and top with the bottled chillies. Serve immediately with the chilli sauce.

tarragon turkey

This economical dish is quick and simple to prepare, and yet it tastes absolutely wonderful, not least because poultry and tarragon have a natural affinity.

INGREDIENTS

4 turkey breasts, about 175 g/6 oz each

salt and pepper

4 tsp wholegrain mustard

8 fresh tarragon sprigs,

plus extra to garnish

4 smoked back bacon rashers

salad leaves, to serve

NUTRITIONAL INFORMATION

Calories	.296
Protein	.48g
Carbohydrate	.0g
Sugars	.1g
Fat	.11g
Saturates	.4g

cook's tip

Make sure that you buy genuine French tarragon, as Russian tarragon is coarse and can taste unpleasant. It is not worth using dried tarragon, which has an insipid flavour.

1 Preheat the barbecue. Season the turkey to taste with salt and pepper, and, using a round-bladed knife, spread the mustard evenly over the turkey.

2 Place 2 tarragon sprigs on top of each turkey breast and wrap a bacon rasher around it to hold the herbs in place. Secure with a cocktail stick.

3 Cook the turkey over medium hot coals for 5–8 minutes on each side. Transfer to serving plates and garnish with tarragon sprigs. Serve with salad leaves.

turkey rolls

🍲 **cook: 30 mins**   🕐 **prep: 20 mins**   **serves 4**

These herb-flavoured rolls conceal a soft centre of melted cheese as a lovely surprise. They are served here with redcurrant relish, but would also be delicious with Mild Mustard Sauce (see page 13).

NUTRITIONAL INFORMATION	
Calories	.430
Protein	.54g
Carbohydrate	.6g
Sugars	.6g
Fat	.21g
Saturates	.9g

INGREDIENTS

2 tbsp sunflower oil

salt and pepper

4 tbsp chopped fresh marjoram

4 turkey breast steaks

4 tsp mild mustard

175 g/6 oz Emmenthal cheese, grated

1 leek, thinly sliced

RELISH

115 g/4 oz redcurrants

2 tbsp chopped fresh mint

2 tsp clear honey

1 tsp red wine vinegar

cook's tip

You can use fresh or thawed frozen redcurrants for the relish. To strip fresh redcurrants from their stalks, simply run the tines of a fork down the length of the stalk over a bowl.

 Preheat the barbecue. To make the redcurrant relish, place all the ingredients in a bowl and mash well with a fork. Season to taste with salt and pepper. Cover with clingfilm and leave to chill in the refrigerator until required.

 Pour the oil into a small bowl, season to taste with pepper and stir in 2 teaspoons of the marjoram. Reserve. Place the turkey steaks between 2 sheets of clingfilm and beat with the side of a rolling pin to flatten. Season with salt and pepper and spread the mustard evenly over them. Divide the cheese, leek and remaining marjoram between the turkey steaks, roll up and tie securely with kitchen string.

3 Brush the turkey rolls with the flavoured oil and cook over medium hot coals, turning and brushing frequently with the remaining oil, for 30 minutes. Serve immediately with the redcurrant relish.

turkey with sun-dried tomato tapenade

cook: 10–15 minutes

prep: 10 mins, plus 1 hr marinating

serves 4

Sun-dried tomatoes have a marvellously rich, fruity flavour which perfectly complements the marinated turkey – making this dish ideal for a hot summer's day.

NUTRITIONAL INFORMATION

Calories 520

Protein 44g

Carbohydrate 4g

Sugars 2g

Fat 34g

Saturates 5g

variation

This dish would also work well with skinless, boneless chicken breasts. Make sure that the chicken is thoroughly cooked before serving.

INGREDIENTS

4 turkey steaks

MARINADE

150 ml/5 fl oz white wine

1 tbsp white wine vinegar

1 tbsp olive oil

1 garlic clove, crushed

1 tbsp chopped fresh parsley

pepper

TAPENADE

225 g/8 oz sun-dried tomatoes in oil, drained

4 canned anchovy fillets, drained

1 garlic clove, crushed

1 tablespoon lemon juice

3 tablespoons chopped fresh parsley

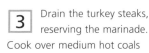

cook's tip

Always marinate the meat in a non-metallic bowl as the marinade usually contains acidic ingredients, such as vinegar or wine. These may react with a metal bowl and taint the flavour of the meat.

1 Place the turkey steaks in a shallow, non-metallic dish. Mix all the marinade ingredients together in a jug, whisking well to mix. Pour the marinade over the turkey steaks, turning to coat. Cover with clingfilm and leave to marinate in the refrigerator for at least 1 hour.

2 Preheat the barbecue. To make the tapenade, put all the ingredients into a food processor and process to a smooth paste. Transfer to a bowl, cover with clingfilm and leave to chill in the refrigerator until required.

3 Drain the turkey steaks, reserving the marinade. Cook over medium hot coals for 10–15 minutes, turning and brushing frequently with the reserved marinade. Transfer to 4 large serving plates and top with the sun-dried tomato tapenade. Serve immediately.

turkey with coriander pesto

serves 4   **prep: 15 mins, plus 2 hrs marinating**   **cook: 10 mins**

Full of Mediterranean flavours, these turkey kebabs would taste fabulous served with a mixed bean salad.

INGREDIENTS

450 g/1 lb skinless, boneless turkey, cut into 5-cm/2-inch cubes

2 courgettes, thickly sliced

1 red and 1 yellow pepper, deseeded and cut into 5-cm/2-inch squares

8 cherry tomatoes

8 baby onions

MARINADE

6 tbsp olive oil

3 tbsp dry white wine

1 tsp green peppercorns, crushed

2 tbsp chopped fresh coriander

salt

CORIANDER PESTO

55 g/2 oz fresh coriander leaves

15 g/½ oz fresh parsley leaves

1 garlic clove

55 g/2 oz pine kernels

25 g/1 oz freshly grated Parmesan cheese

6 tbsp extra virgin olive oil

juice of 1 lemon

NUTRITIONAL INFORMATION

Calories 596

Protein 33g

Carbohydrate 11g

Sugars 8g

Fat 46g

Saturates 7g

variation

Substitute Parma ham for the bacon and for a traditional pesto, replace the coriander leaves with the same amount of fresh basil leaves.

cook's tip

It is best to use freeze-dried green peppercorns rather than the bottled variety, which tend to taste heavily of vinegar. If you do use bottled ones, drain and rinse before using.

1 Place the turkey in a large glass bowl. To make the marinade, mix the olive oil, wine, peppercorns and coriander together in a jug and season to taste with salt. Pour the mixture over the turkey and turn until the turkey is thoroughly coated. Cover with clingfilm and leave to marinate in the refrigerator for 2 hours.

2 Preheat the barbecue. To make the pesto, put the coriander and parsley into a food processor and process until finely chopped. Add the garlic and pine kernels and pulse until chopped. Add the Parmesan cheese, oil and lemon juice and process briefly to mix. Transfer to a bowl, cover and leave to chill in the refrigerator until required.

3 Drain the turkey, reserving the marinade. Thread the turkey, courgette slices, pepper pieces, cherry tomatoes and onions alternately on to metal skewers. Cook over medium hot coals, turning and brushing frequently with the marinade, for 10 minutes. Serve immediately with the coriander pesto.

fruity duck

⏲ **cook: 12–16 mins**   ⏱ **prep: 10 minutes**   **serves 4**

Apricots and onions counteract the richness of the duck. Its high fat content makes it virtually self-basting, so it stays superbly moist. The duck looks particularly elegant garnished with spring onion tassels.

INGREDIENTS

4 duck breasts

115 g/4 oz ready-to-eat dried apricots

2 shallots, thinly sliced

2 tbsp clear honey

1 tsp sesame oil

2 tsp Chinese five-spice powder

4 spring onions, to garnish

variation

Substitute 4 pork chops for the duck and cook over medium hot coals for 8–9 minutes on each side, or until thoroughly cooked.

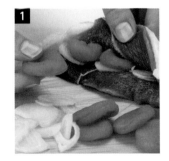

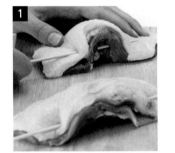

cook's tip

Available from Chinese supermarkets, Chinese five-spice powder contains finely ground Sichuan pepper, cassia, fennel seed, star anise and cloves. It is not the same as Indian five-spice powder.

1 Preheat the barbecue. Using a sharp knife, cut a long slit in the fleshy side of each duck breast to make a pocket. Divide the apricots and shallots between the pockets and secure with skewers.

2 Mix the honey and sesame oil together in a small bowl and brush all over the duck. Sprinkle with the

Chinese five-spice powder. To make the garnish, make a few cuts lengthways down the stem of each spring onion. Place in a bowl of ice-cold water and leave until the tassels open out. Drain well before using.

3 Cook the duck over medium hot coals for 6–8 minutes on each side.

Remove the skewers, transfer to a large serving plate and garnish with the spring onion tassels. Serve immediately.

butterflied poussins

serves 4

prep: 20 mins, plus 8 hrs marinating ⏲

cook: 25–30 mins ⏲

The poussins are coated in a thick mustard paste, which not only gives them a tantalizingly delicious flavour, but also turns them a lovely orange-gold colour.

INGREDIENTS

4 poussins, about 450 g/1 lb each

1 tbsp paprika

1 tbsp mustard powder

1 tbsp ground cumin

pinch of cayenne pepper

1 tbsp tomato ketchup

1 tbsp lemon juice

salt

5 tbsp melted butter

fresh coriander sprigs, to garnish

NUTRITIONAL INFORMATION

Calories 583

Protein 40g

Carbohydrate 3g

Sugars 2g

Fat 41g

Saturates 17g

variation

Substitute quail for the poussins. Quail are smaller than poussins, weighing 115–140 g/4–5 oz, so you will need 8 birds. Cook for 15–20 minutes.

cook's tip

Keep a close watch on the poussins while cooking and if they look as if they are drying out, brush with a little sunflower oil.

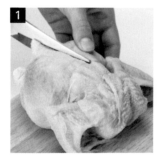

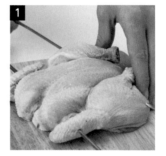

1 To spatchcock the poussins, turn 1 bird breast-side down and, using strong kitchen scissors or poultry shears, cut through the skin and ribcage along both sides of the backbone, from tail to neck. Remove the backbone and turn the bird breast-side up. Press down firmly on the breastbone to flatten. Fold the wingtips underneath. Push a skewer through one wing, the top of the breast and out of the other wing. Push a second skewer through one thigh, the bottom of the breast and out through the other thigh. Repeat with the remaining poussins.

2 Mix the paprika, mustard powder, cumin, cayenne, tomato ketchup and lemon juice together in a small bowl and season to taste with salt. Gradually stir in the butter to make a smooth paste. Spread the paste evenly over the poussins, cover and leave to marinate in the refrigerator for up to 8 hours.

3 Preheat the barbecue. Cook the poussins over medium hot coals, turning frequently, for 25–30 minutes, brushing with a little oil if necessary. Transfer to a serving plate, garnish with fresh coriander sprigs and serve.

chicken livers with sweet & sour relish

cook: 10 mins **prep: 15 mins** **serves 4**

NUTRITIONAL INFORMATION

Calories	.315
Protein	.24g
Carbohydrate	.28g
Sugars	.27g
Fat	.13g
Saturates	.4g

variation

Other vegetables would also work well, such as small strips of red or orange pepper and courgette batons instead of the button mushrooms.

Both liver and bacon and prunes and bacon are well-known combinations, and here they are mixed with cherry tomatoes and mushrooms and served with a savoury relish for a taste sensation.

INGREDIENTS

350 g/12 oz chicken livers

115 g/4 oz streaky bacon
rashers, rinded

8 no-soak dried prunes

8 cherry tomatoes

8 button mushrooms

sunflower oil, for brushing

SWEET & SOUR RELISH

5 tbsp sweet pickle

3 tbsp tomato ketchup

3 tbsp brown sauce

4½ tsp cider vinegar

4½ tsp Worcestershire sauce

cook's tip

Dried no-soak fruit is the same as the dried, but moist, ready-to-eat fruit. It is available in health food shops and most supermarkets.

1 Preheat the barbecue. To make the relish, place all the ingredients in a bowl and mix together. Cover with clingfilm and reserve until required.

2 Rinse the chicken livers in cold water and pat dry with kitchen paper. Cut the bacon rashers in half. Wrap a piece of bacon around each chicken liver and secure with a cocktail stick. Wrap a prune around the base of each tomato. Thread the chicken livers, prune-wrapped tomatoes and mushrooms on to presoaked wooden skewers and brush with oil.

3 Cook over medium hot coals for 5 minutes on each side. Remove the skewers, transfer to a large serving plate and serve immediately with the relish.

meat

For many people, barbecues mean plenty of meat and this chapter will not disappoint them. Steaks, chops, ribs, kebabs, sausages and burgers appear in many guises, from fragrant lamb in Rack & Ruin (see page 102) to bacon-wrapped sausages in Pigs in Blankets (see page 121). Popular barbecue favourites include Beef Satay (see page 97), Shashlik (see page 110) and Chinese Ribs (see page 115), while more unusual dishes range from Sozzled Lamb Chops (see page 112) to Meatballs on Sticks (see page 118). Those with a hearty appetite might like to tackle Easy Mixed Grill (see page 122), while anyone who has ever been disappointed by ready-made hamburgers – and who hasn't? – will love Best-ever Burgers (see page 90).

Marinades are a very important aspect of preparing meat for the barbecue, as they often help to tenderize it to a melt-in-the-mouth texture. Ideally, prepare the ingredients the night before the barbecue and let the meat marinate overnight in the refrigerator. This also allows the flavours to mingle and permeate the meat. Recipes range from hot and spicy to cool and minty, and from sophisticated and subtle to robust and hearty.

As with the poultry recipes, you can mix and match the sauces or use one from the beginning of the book. Try serving Tabasco Steaks (see page 92) with Guacamole (see page 13) instead of Watercress Butter for example, or Tomato Relish (see page 94) with Spicy Lamb Steaks (see page 104). Experiment and enjoy.

best-ever burgers

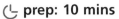

 cook: 6–8 mins   **prep: 10 mins**   **serves 6**

NUTRITIONAL INFORMATION

Calories 659

Protein 44g

Carbohydrate 66g

Sugars 8g

Fat 26g

Saturates 5g

variation

For Tex-Mex burgers, add 2 deseeded and finely chopped fresh green chillies to the mixture in Step 1 and serve with Guacamole (see page 13).

Barbecues and burgers are almost inseparable. However, these succulent, home-made burgers bear no resemblance to the little ready-made patties available in most shops.

INGREDIENTS

900 g/2 lb lean minced steak

2 onions, finely chopped

25 g/1 oz fresh white breadcrumbs

1 egg, lightly beaten

1½ teaspoons finely chopped
fresh thyme

salt and pepper

TO SERVE

6 sesame seed baps

2 tomatoes

1 onion

lettuce leaves

Mayonnaise (see page 13)

mustard

tomato ketchup

cook's tip

Home-made burgers have a much looser texture than ready-made ones, so use a fish slice to turn them carefully and remove from the barbecue as soon as they are cooked.

1 Preheat the barbecue. Place the steak, onions, breadcrumbs, egg and thyme in a large glass bowl and season to taste with salt and pepper. Mix thoroughly using your hands.

2 Form the mixture into 6 large patties with your hands and a round-bladed knife.

3 Cook the burgers over hot coals for 3–4 minutes on each side. Meanwhile, cut the baps in half and briefly toast on the barbecue, cut-side down. Using a sharp knife, slice the tomatoes and cut the onion into thinly sliced rings. Fill the toasted baps with the cooked burgers, lettuce, sliced tomatoes and onion rings and

serve immediately, with the Mayonnaise, mustard and tomato ketchup.

tabasco steaks with watercress butter

serves 4 | **prep: 10 mins** | **cook: 5–12 mins**

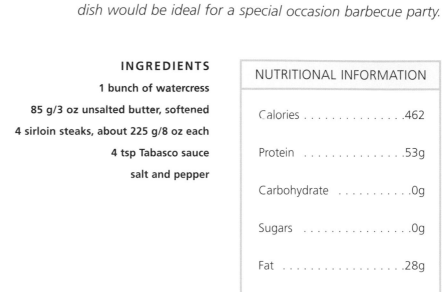

A variation on a classic theme, this simple, but rather extravagant dish would be ideal for a special occasion barbecue party.

INGREDIENTS

1 bunch of watercress

85 g/3 oz unsalted butter, softened

4 sirloin steaks, about 225 g/8 oz each

4 tsp Tabasco sauce

salt and pepper

NUTRITIONAL INFORMATION

Calories 462

Protein 53g

Carbohydrate 0g

Sugars 0g

Fat 28g

Saturates 16g

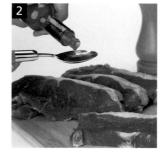

variation

If you like, substitute the same amount of fresh parsley for the watercress. Alternatively, serve the steaks with Coriander Pesto (see page 80).

1 Preheat the barbecue. Using a sharp knife, finely chop enough watercress to fill 4 tablespoons. Reserve a few watercress leaves for the garnish. Place the butter in a small bowl and beat in the chopped watercress with a fork until fully incorporated. Cover with clingfilm and leave to chill in the refrigerator until required.

2 Sprinkle each steak with 1 teaspoon of the Tabasco sauce, rubbing it in well. Season to taste with salt and pepper.

3 Cook the steaks over hot coals for 2½ minutes each side for rare, 4 minutes each side for medium and 6 minutes each side for well done. Transfer to

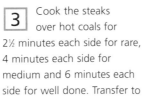

serving plates, garnish with the reserved watercress leaves and serve immediately, topped with the watercress butter.

steak parcels

cook: 10 mins

prep: 10 mins, plus 8 hrs marinating

serves 4

A red wine marinade is perfect for steak, as it imparts a delicious flavour and tenderises the meat to a melt-in-the-mouth consistency.

NUTRITIONAL INFORMATION

Calories	.466
Protein	.54g
Carbohydrate	.3g
Sugars	.2g
Fat	.21g
Saturates	.9g

INGREDIENTS

4 sirloin or rump steaks

300 ml/10 fl oz dry red wine

2 tbsp olive oil

salt and pepper

25 g/1 oz butter

2 tsp Dijon mustard

4 shallots, finely chopped

4 fresh thyme sprigs

4 bay leaves

variation

If you like, substitute the same amount of creamed horseradish for the mustard and use fresh marjoram sprigs instead of the thyme.

1 Place the steaks in a large, shallow, non-metallic dish. Mix the wine and oil together in a jug and season to taste with salt and pepper. Pour the marinade over the steaks, cover with clingfilm and leave to marinate in the refrigerator for up to 8 hours.

2 Preheat the barbecue. Cut out 4 squares of foil large enough to enclose the steaks and coat the centres with the butter and mustard. Drain the steaks and place them on the foil squares. Top with the shallots, thyme and bay leaves and fold over the foil to make neat parcels.

3 Cook the parcels over hot coals for 10 minutes, turning once. Serve the steaks immediately in the parcels.

mustard steaks with tomato relish

serves 4   **prep: 10 mins, plus** ⏲   **cook: 50–60 mins** ⏲
1 hr cooling/standing

Tarragon mustard gives these steaks a subtle spicy flavour that contrasts well with the sharp taste of the sweet-and-sour tomato relish. Serve with a salad and potatoes for a filling main course.

INGREDIENTS

4 sirloin or rump steaks

1 tbsp tarragon mustard

2 garlic cloves, crushed

fresh tarragon sprigs, to garnish

TOMATO RELISH

225 g/8 oz cherry tomatoes

55 g/2 oz muscovado sugar

50 ml/2 fl oz white wine vinegar

1 piece of stem ginger, chopped

½ lime, thinly sliced

salt

NUTRITIONAL INFORMATION

Calories	.380
Protein	.54g
Carbohydrate	.18g
Sugars	.17g
Fat	.11g
Saturates	.5g

---

variation

Substitute a different flavoured mustard – there is a huge variety available these days, including chilli, honey, whisky and Champagne flavour.

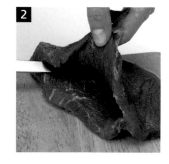

cook's tip

Use long-handled tongs to turn the steaks over. Try to avoid using a fork as this will pierce the meat and some of the delicious juices will be lost.

1 To make the tomato relish, place all the ingredients in a heavy-based saucepan, seasoning to taste with salt. Bring to the boil, stirring until the sugar has completely dissolved. Reduce the heat and simmer, stirring occasionally, for 40 minutes, or until thickened. Transfer to a bowl, cover with clingfilm and leave to cool.

2 Preheat the barbecue. Using a sharp knife, cut almost completely through each steak horizontally to make a pocket. Spread the mustard inside the pockets and rub the steaks all over with the garlic. Place them on a plate, cover with clingfilm and leave to stand for 30 minutes.

3 Cook the steaks over hot coals for 2½ minutes each side for rare, 4 minutes each side for medium or 6 minutes each side for well done. Transfer to serving plates, garnish with fresh tarragon sprigs and serve immediately with the tomato relish.

luxury cheeseburgers

serves 4　　　　**prep: 15 mins** ⏲　　　　**cook: 10 mins** ⏲

This is a sophisticated version of the traditional burger with a surprise filling of melted blue cheese. Serve with plenty of salad leaves to make a substantial barbecue lunch.

INGREDIENTS

55 g/2 oz Stilton cheese

450 g/1 lb lean minced steak

1 onion, finely chopped

1 celery stick, finely chopped

1 tsp creamed horseradish

1 tbsp chopped fresh thyme

salt and pepper

TO SERVE

4 sesame seed baps

lettuce leaves

sliced tomatoes

NUTRITIONAL INFORMATION	
Calories	.360
Protein	.32g
Carbohydrate	.32g
Sugars	.4g
Fat	.13g
Saturates	.5g

variation

Substitute Wensleydale or Lancashire cheese for the Stilton and finely snipped chives for the thyme.

1 Preheat the barbecue. Crumble the Stilton into a bowl and reserve until required. Place the steak, onion, celery, horseradish and thyme in a separate bowl and season to taste with salt and pepper. Mix thoroughly using your hands.

2 Form the mixture into 8 patties with your hands and a round-bladed knife. Divide the cheese between 4 of them and top with the remaining patties. Gently press them together and mould the edges.

3 Cook the burgers over hot coals for 5 minutes on each side. Meanwhile, cut the baps in half and briefly toast on the barbecue, cut-side down. Fill the baps with the cooked burgers, lettuce and tomato slices and serve immediately.

beef satay

cook: 5–8 mins

prep: 10 mins, plus 2 hrs marinating

serves 6

Many Westerners assume that a satay must involve a peanut sauce, but this is not always true. The term simply refers to a kebab that has been marinated in a flavoursome mixture of any kind.

NUTRITIONAL INFORMATION

Calories	.258
Protein	.37g
Carbohydrate	.4g
Sugars	.3g
Fat	.11g
Saturates	.4g

INGREDIENTS

1 kg/2 lb 4 oz rump steak

1 tbsp clear honey

2 tbsp dark soy sauce

2 tbsp groundnut oil

1 garlic clove, finely chopped

1 tsp ground coriander

1 tsp caraway seeds

pinch of chilli powder

lime wedges, to garnish

cook's tip

Instead of cutting the steak into small cubes, slice it into long narrow strips and thread the strips in zigzags on to the skewers.

1 Using a sharp knife, cut the steak into 2.5-cm/ 1-inch cubes, then place in a large, shallow, non-metallic dish. Mix the honey, soy sauce, oil, garlic, coriander, caraway seeds and chilli powder together in a small jug. Pour the mixture over the steak and stir until the steak is thoroughly coated with the marinade. Cover with clingfilm and leave to marinate in the refrigerator for 2 hours, turning occasionally.

2 Preheat the barbecue. Drain the steak, reserving the marinade. Thread the steak on to several presoaked wooden skewers.

3 Cook the steak over hot coals, turning and brushing frequently with the reserved marinade, for 5–8 minutes. Transfer to a large serving plate, garnish with lime wedges and serve.

beef, lamb & bacon brochettes

serves 4   **prep: 15 mins** ⏲   **cook: 15–20 mins** 🍲

This is a veritable feast for meat-lovers – satisfying, easy to prepare skewers, served with a rich tomato sauce.

INGREDIENTS

400 g/14 oz rump steak, cut into
2.5-cm/1-inch cubes

400 g/14 oz boneless leg of lamb, cut
into 2.5-cm/1-inch cubes

8 back bacon rashers, rinded and
cut into thin strips

8 shallots, halved

8 tomatoes, halved

12 bottled chillies, drained

4 tbsp sunflower oil

4 garlic cloves, finely chopped

2 tsp paprika

¼ tsp cayenne pepper

TOMATO SAUCE

225 g/8 oz tomatoes, peeled
and chopped

1 onion, finely chopped

1 green pepper, deseeded and
finely chopped

3 tbsp finely chopped fresh parsley

3 tbsp tomato ketchup

pinch of sugar

pinch of chilli powder

salt and pepper

NUTRITIONAL INFORMATION

Calories 675

Protein 59g

Carbohydrate 18g

Sugars 15g

Fat 42g

Saturates 14g

---

variation

Other vegetables would be suitable to use as part of the kebabs, such as onion wedges and small strips of red or yellow pepper.

cook's tip

Make sure that the skewers you use are long enough and try not to overcrowd them on the barbecue rack, otherwise the food will not cook evenly. If space is a problem, cook the brochettes in batches.

1 Preheat the barbecue. To make the tomato sauce, rub the tomatoes through a fine sieve into a small bowl, then stir in the onion, green pepper, parsley, tomato ketchup and sugar and season to taste with chilli powder, salt and pepper. Cover with clingfilm and leave to chill in the refrigerator until required.

2 Thread the steak, lamb, bacon, shallots, tomatoes and chillies alternately on to 4 metal or presoaked wooden skewers. Mix the oil, garlic, paprika and cayenne together in a small bowl. Brush the brochettes with the oil.

3 Cook the brochettes over medium hot coals, turning and brushing frequently with the spicy oil, for 15–20 minutes. Transfer to a large serving plate and serve immediately with the tomato sauce.

indonesian beef kebabs

cook: 10 mins

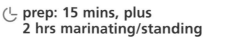 prep: 15 mins, plus
2 hrs marinating/standing

serves 4

NUTRITIONAL INFORMATION

Calories 175

Protein 26g

Carbohydrate 8g

Sugars 6g

Fat 5g

Saturates 2g

These spicy Indonesian kebabs are traditionally served with sambal kecap – a delicious chilli-flavoured dipping sauce – and a refreshing cucumber salad.

INGREDIENTS

1 tsp coriander seeds

½ tsp cumin seeds

450 g/1 lb rump steak cut into strips

1 onion

2 garlic cloves

1 tbsp muscovado sugar

1 tbsp dark soy sauce

4 tbsp lemon juice

salt

SAUCE

1 fresh red chilli

4 tbsp dark soy sauce

2 garlic cloves, finely chopped

4 tsp lemon juice

2 tbsp hot water

variation

Add extra hotness to the sauce by using 1–2 very hot fresh bird's eye chillies. Remember to wash your hands thoroughly after chopping.

cook's tip

If you don't have a mortar and pestle handy, then you can grind the coriander and cumin seeds in a spice mill or even a clean coffee grinder.

1 To make the sauce, using a sharp knife, deseed the chilli and finely chop. Place in a small bowl with all the other sauce ingredients and mix together. Cover with clingfilm and leave to stand until required.

2 Dry-fry the coriander and cumin seeds in a frying pan for 1 minute, or until they give off their aroma and begin to pop. Remove from the heat and grind in a mortar with a pestle. Place the steak in a shallow, non-metallic dish and add the ground spices, stirring to coat. Put the onion, garlic, sugar, soy sauce and lemon juice into a food processor and process to a paste. Season to taste with salt and spoon the mixture over

the steak, turning to coat. Cover with clingfilm and leave to marinate in the refrigerator for 2 hours.

3 Preheat the barbecue. Drain the steak, reserving the marinade, and thread it on to several presoaked wooden or metal skewers. Cook over hot coals, turning and basting frequently

with the reserved marinade, for 5–8 minutes, until thoroughly cooked. Transfer to a large serving plate and serve with the sauce for dipping.

rack & ruin

serves 4   **prep: 10 mins, plus 1 hr marinating**   **cook: 20 mins**

This quick and easy dish is perfect for serving as part of a summer party menu, along with plenty of salad and potatoes.

INGREDIENTS

4 racks of lamb, each with 4 cutlets

2 tbsp extra virgin olive oil

1 tbsp balsamic vinegar

1 tbsp lemon juice

3 tbsp finely chopped fresh rosemary

1 small onion, finely chopped

salt and pepper

NUTRITIONAL INFORMATION	
Calories	798
Protein	46g
Carbohydrate	2g
Sugars	1g
Fat	68g
Saturates	31g

1 Place the racks of lamb in a large, shallow, non-metallic dish. Place the oil, vinegar, lemon juice, rosemary and onion in a jug and stir together. Season to taste with salt and pepper.

2 Pour the marinade over the lamb and turn until thoroughly coated. Cover with clingfilm and leave to marinate in the refrigerator for 1 hour, turning occasionally.

3 Preheat the barbecue. Drain the racks of lamb, reserving the marinade. Cook over medium hot coals, brushing frequently with the marinade, for 10 minutes on each side. Serve immediately.

cook's tip

Balsamic vinegar is a smooth, mellow-flavoured dark vinegar made in the region surrounding Modena in northern Italy. It is quite expensive, but has a unique flavour.

soy pork with coriander

cook: 14–20 mins

prep: 10 mins, plus 1 hr marinating

serves 4

The spicy, Eastern-style flavours that suffuse these pork chops will make them an unusual and original barbecue favourite.

NUTRITIONAL INFORMATION	
Calories	.469
Protein	.40g
Carbohydrate	.3g
Sugars	.1g
Fat	.33g
Saturates	.12g

INGREDIENTS

4 pork chops, about 175 g/6 oz each

1 tbsp coriander seeds

6 black peppercorns

4 tbsp dark soy sauce

1 garlic clove, finely chopped

1 tsp sugar

fresh coriander sprigs, to garnish

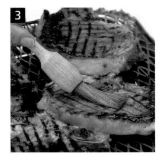

cook's tip

It is worth taking the time to find a good-quality soy sauce for the aromatic marinade that flavours these chops. Chinese supermarkets stock the best range of sauces.

1 Place the pork chops in a large, shallow, non-metallic dish. Crush the coriander seeds and peppercorns in a spice mill. Alternatively, place in a mortar and crush with a pestle. Place the soy sauce, garlic, sugar, crushed coriander seeds and peppercorns in a jug and stir well until the sugar has dissolved.

2 Pour the soy sauce mixture over the chops, turning to coat. Cover with clingfilm and leave to marinate in the refrigerator for 1 hour, turning occasionally.

3 Preheat the barbecue. Drain the chops, reserving the marinade. Cook over medium hot coals, brushing frequently with the reserved marinade, for 7–10 minutes on each side. Transfer to a large serving plate, garnish with fresh coriander sprigs and serve.

spicy lamb steaks

cook: 40 mins

prep: 15 mins, plus 3 hrs 20 mins cooling/marinating   serves 4

Lamb, fresh rosemary and bay leaves always go so well together, and in this delicious dish a hot and spicy marinade is used to give the lamb an extra special flavour.

NUTRITIONAL INFORMATION

Calories 490

Protein 39g

Carbohydrate 23g

Sugars 20g

Fat 28g

Saturates 9g

variation

Many different marinades will work equally well for this lamb dish. Try a White Wine Marinade or a Hot Pepper Marinade (see page 13).

INGREDIENTS

4 lamb steaks, about 175 g/6 oz each

8 fresh rosemary sprigs

8 fresh bay leaves

2 tbsp olive oil

SPICY MARINADE

2 tbsp sunflower oil

1 large onion, finely chopped

2 garlic cloves, finely chopped

2 tbsp jerk seasoning

1 tbsp curry paste

1 tsp grated fresh root ginger

400 g/14 oz canned chopped tomatoes

4 tbsp Worcestershire sauce

3 tbsp light muscovado sugar

salt and pepper

cook's tip

You can buy ready-made jerk seasoning at most supermarkets. Alternatively, make your own, following Step 1 of the recipe for Jerk Chicken on page 61.

1 To make the marinade, heat the oil in a heavy-based saucepan. Add the onion and garlic and cook, stirring occasionally, for 5 minutes, or until softened. Stir in the jerk seasoning, curry paste and grated ginger and cook, stirring constantly, for 2 minutes. Add the tomatoes, Worcestershire sauce and sugar, then season to taste

with salt and pepper. Bring to the boil, stirring constantly, then reduce the heat and simmer for 15 minutes, or until thickened. Remove from the heat and leave to cool.

2 Place the lamb steaks between 2 sheets of clingfilm and beat with the side of a rolling pin to flatten. Transfer the steaks to a large,

shallow, non-metallic dish. Pour the marinade over them, turning to coat. Cover with clingfilm and leave to marinate in the refrigerator for 3 hours.

3 Preheat the barbecue. Drain the lamb, reserving the marinade. Cook the lamb over medium hot coals, brushing frequently with the marinade, for 5–7 minutes

on each side. Meanwhile, dip the rosemary and bay leaves in the olive oil and cook on the barbecue for 3–5 minutes. Serve the lamb immediately with the herbs.

minted lamb chops

serves 6   **prep: 15 mins, plus 2 hrs marinating**   **cook: 10–14 mins**

You can prepare this dish with any kind of lamb chops – leg chops are especially tender – or cutlets, in which case you will probably require two per serving. Shoulder steaks also work well.

INGREDIENTS

6 chump chops, about 175 g/6 oz each

150 ml/5 fl oz natural Greek yogurt

2 garlic cloves, finely chopped

1 tsp grated fresh root ginger

¼ tsp coriander seeds, crushed

salt and pepper

1 tbsp olive oil, plus extra for brushing

1 tbsp orange juice

1 tsp walnut oil

2 tbsp chopped fresh mint

NUTRITIONAL INFORMATION	
Calories	.420
Protein	.30g
Carbohydrate	.1g
Sugars	.1g
Fat	.33g
Saturates	.15g

variation

If you like, omit the orange juice and walnut oil and stir in ¼ teaspoon ground star anise and a pinch each of ground cinnamon and ground cumin.

1 Place the chops in a large, shallow, non-metallic bowl. Mix half the yogurt, the garlic, ginger and coriander seeds together in a jug and season to taste with salt and pepper. Spoon the mixture over the chops, turning to coat, then cover with clingfilm and leave to marinate in the refrigerator for 2 hours, turning occasionally.

2 Preheat the barbecue. Place the remaining yogurt, the olive oil, orange juice, walnut oil and mint in a small bowl and, using a hand-held whisk, whisk until thoroughly blended. Season to taste with salt and pepper. Cover the minted yogurt with clingfilm and leave to chill in the refrigerator until ready to serve.

3 Drain the chops, scraping off the marinade. Brush with olive oil and cook over medium hot coals for 5–7 minutes on each side. Serve immediately with the minted yogurt.

normandy brochettes

cook: 12–15 mins   **prep: 10 mins, plus 1–2 hrs marinating**   **serves 4**

The orchards of Normandy are famous throughout France, providing both eating apples and cider-making varieties. For an authentic touch, enjoy a glass of Calvados between courses.

NUTRITIONAL INFORMATION	
Calories	.242
Protein	.24g
Carbohydrate	.8g
Sugars	.8g
Fat	.11g
Saturates	.3g

INGREDIENTS

450 g/1 lb pork fillet

300 ml/10 fl oz dry cider

1 tbsp finely chopped fresh sage

6 black peppercorns, crushed

2 crisp eating apples

1 tbsp sunflower oil

variation

Replace 1 apple with 6 no-soak dried prunes wrapped in strips of streaky bacon. Thread the prunes on to the skewers with the remaining apple and pork.

1 Using a sharp knife, cut the pork into 2.5-cm/1-inch cubes, then place in a large, shallow, non-metallic dish. Mix the cider, sage and peppercorns together in a jug, pour the mixture over the pork and turn until thoroughly coated. Cover with clingfilm and leave to marinate in the refrigerator for 1–2 hours.

2 Preheat the barbecue. Drain the pork, reserving the marinade. Core the apples, but do not peel, then cut into wedges. Dip the apple wedges into the reserved marinade and thread on to several metal skewers, alternating with the cubes of pork. Stir the sunflower oil into the remaining marinade.

3 Cook the brochettes over medium hot coals, turning and brushing frequently with the reserved marinade, for 12–15 minutes. Transfer to a large serving plate and if you prefer, remove the meat and apples from the skewers before serving. Serve immediately.

turkish kebabs

serves 4   prep: 20 mins, plus 2 hrs marinating   cook: 10–15 mins

Turkey, the bridge between East and West, has an eclectic mix of influences in its cooking style. These traditional kebabs would originally have been made with mutton or, possibly, young goat.

INGREDIENTS

500 g/1 lb 2 oz boned shoulder of
lamb, cut into 2.5-cm/1-inch cubes

1 tbsp olive oil

2 tbsp dry white wine

2 tbsp finely chopped fresh mint

4 garlic cloves, finely chopped

2 tsp grated orange rind

1 tbsp paprika

1 tsp sugar

salt and pepper

TAHINI CREAM

225 g/8 oz tahini paste

2 garlic cloves, finely chopped

2 tbsp extra virgin olive oil

2 tbsp lemon juice

125 ml/4 fl oz water

NUTRITIONAL INFORMATION

Calories 752

Protein 43g

Carbohydrate 2g

Sugars 1g

Fat 63g

Saturates 16g

variation

You can also serve these kebabs with other sauces, such as Tsatziki (see page 153) or even a Tomato Sauce (see page 98).

cook's tip

Tahini or sesame seed paste is available from most supermarkets and specialist food shops. It is made from ground, pulped sesame seeds.

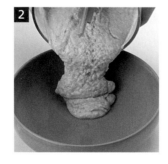

1 Place the lamb cubes in a large, shallow, non-metallic dish. Mix the olive oil, wine, mint, garlic, orange rind, paprika and sugar together in a jug and season to taste with salt and pepper. Pour the mixture over the lamb, turning to coat, then cover with clingfilm and leave to marinate in the refrigerator for 2 hours, turning occasionally.

2 Preheat the barbecue. To make the tahini cream, put the tahini paste, garlic, oil and lemon juice into a food processor and process briefly to mix. With the motor still running, gradually add the water through the feeder tube until smooth. Transfer to a bowl, cover with clingfilm and leave to chill in the refrigerator until required.

3 Drain the lamb, reserving the marinade, and thread it on to several long metal skewers. Cook over medium hot coals, turning and brushing frequently with the reserved marinade, for 10–15 minutes. Serve with the tahini cream.

shashlik

cook: 10–15 mins

prep: 20 mins, plus 8 hrs marinating

serves 4

variation

It you like, you can use other marinades to flavour the lamb, such as White Wine Marinade (see page 13).

Fragrant, lemon–flavoured kebabs, shashlik are a Georgian speciality from the fertile area between the Black Sea and the Caucasian Mountains in the Russian Federation. They have much in common with neighbouring Turkey's shish kebabs.

INGREDIENTS

675 g/1 lb 8 oz boneless leg of lamb, cut into 2.5-cm/1-inch cubes

12 large mushrooms

4 streaky bacon rashers, rinded

8 cherry tomatoes

1 large green pepper, deseeded and cut into squares

fresh herb sprigs, to garnish

MARINADE

4 tbsp sunflower oil

4 tbsp lemon juice

1 onion, finely chopped

½ tsp dried rosemary

½ tsp dried thyme

salt and pepper

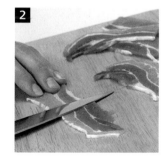

cook's tip

When barbecuing all types of kebabs, make sure that they are brushed with the marinade or oil and turned frequently, otherwise they may burn.

1 Place the lamb and mushrooms in a large, shallow, non-metallic dish. Mix all the ingredients for the marinade together in a jug, seasoning to taste with salt and pepper. Pour the mixture over the lamb and mushrooms, turning to coat. Cover with clingfilm and leave to marinate in the refrigerator for up to 8 hours.

2 Preheat the barbecue. Cut the bacon rashers in half across the centre and stretch with a heavy, flat-bladed knife, then roll up. Drain the lamb and mushrooms, reserving the marinade. Thread the bacon rolls, lamb, mushrooms, tomatoes and green pepper squares alternately on to metal skewers. Sieve the marinade.

3 Cook the kebabs over medium hot coals, turning and brushing frequently with the reserved marinade, for 10–15 minutes. Transfer to a large serving plate, garnish with fresh herb sprigs and serve immediately.

sozzled lamb chops

serves 4   **prep: 15 mins, plus 5 mins marinating** ⏲   **cook: 10 mins** ♨

These chops will only need marinating for a short time, as the marinade is quite strongly flavoured. They are delicious served with a rich, tasty mustard butter.

INGREDIENTS

8 lamb loin chops

fresh parsley sprigs, to garnish

salad, to serve

MARINADE

2 tbsp extra virgin olive oil

2 tbsp Worcestershire sauce

2 tbsp lemon juice

2 tbsp dry gin

1 garlic clove, finely chopped

salt and pepper

MUSTARD BUTTER

55 g/2 oz unsalted butter, softened

1½ tsp tarragon mustard

1 tbsp chopped fresh parsley

dash of lemon juice

NUTRITIONAL INFORMATION

Calories 770

Protein 52g

Carbohydrate 2g

Sugars 1g

Fat 60g

Saturates 29g

variation

Instead of mustard butter, serve the chops with Watercress Butter (see page 92) and garnish with fresh watercress instead of parsley.

cook's tip

Make sure that the barbecue has reached the correct temperature before cooking, otherwise you will only blacken the food on the outside and the inside will still be raw.

1 Preheat the barbecue. Place the lamb chops in a large, shallow, non-metallic dish. Mix all the ingredients for the marinade together in a jug, seasoning to taste with salt and pepper. Pour the mixture over the chops and then turn them until they are thoroughly coated. Cover with clingfilm and leave to marinate for 5 minutes.

2 To make the mustard butter, mix all the ingredients together in a small bowl, beating with a fork until well blended. Cover with clingfilm and leave to chill in the refrigerator until required.

3 Drain the chops, reserving the marinade. Cook over medium hot coals, brushing frequently with the reserved marinade, for 5 minutes on each side. Transfer to serving plates, top with the mustard butter and garnish with parsley sprigs. Serve immediately with salad.

hot & spicy ribs

serves 4   **prep: 15 mins**   **cook: 1 hr**

Twice-cooked (first in the kitchen and then on the barbecue), these succulent, pork spare ribs are deliciously tender and packed full of spicy flavours.

INGREDIENTS

1 onion, chopped

2 garlic cloves, chopped

2.5-cm/1-inch piece fresh root ginger, sliced

1 fresh red chilli, deseeded and chopped

5 tbsp dark soy sauce

3 tbsp lime juice

1 tbsp palm or muscovado sugar

2 tbsp groundnut oil

salt and pepper

1 kg/2 lb 4 oz pork spare ribs, separated

NUTRITIONAL INFORMATION	
Calories	.466
Protein	.38g
Carbohydrate	.11g
Sugars	.7g
Fat	.30g
Saturates	.10g

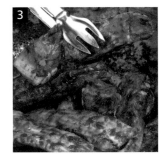

cook's tip

Groundnut oil is used extensively in South-east Asian cooking. It is usually available in most large supermarkets, but if you cannot find it, then use sunflower oil instead.

1 Preheat the barbecue. Put the onion, garlic, ginger, chilli and soy sauce into a food processor and process to a paste. Transfer to a jug and stir in the lime juice, sugar and oil and season to taste with salt and pepper.

2 Place the spare ribs in a preheated wok or large, heavy-based saucepan and pour in the soy sauce mixture. Place on the hob and bring to the boil, then simmer over a low heat, stirring frequently, for 30 minutes. If the mixture appears to be drying out, add a little water.

3 Remove the spare ribs, reserving the sauce. Cook the ribs over medium hot coals, turning and basting frequently with the sauce, for 20–30 minutes. Transfer to a large serving plate and serve immediately.

chinese ribs

cook: 30–40 mins   **prep: 10 mins, plus 6 hrs marinating**   **serves 4**

Leave these pork spare ribs to marinate for as long as possible to ensure that the wonderful flavours of the marinade mingle and thoroughly permeate the meat.

NUTRITIONAL INFORMATION	
Calories	450
Protein	38g
Carbohydrate	14g
Sugars	12g
Fat	27g
Saturates	9g

INGREDIENTS

1 kg/2 lb 4 oz pork spare
ribs, separated

4 tbsp dark soy sauce

3 tbsp muscovado sugar

1 tbsp groundnut or sunflower oil

2 garlic cloves, finely chopped

2 tsp Chinese five-spice powder

1-cm/½-inch piece fresh root
ginger, grated

shredded spring onions, to garnish

variation

Marinate the meat in 4 tablespoons each soy sauce and honey, 1 tablespoon water, 1 teaspoon mustard powder and a pinch of cayenne pepper.

1 Place the spare ribs in a large, shallow, non-metallic dish. Mix the soy sauce, sugar, oil, garlic, Chinese five-spice powder and ginger together in a bowl. Pour the mixture over the ribs and turn until the ribs are thoroughly coated in the marinade.

2 Cover the dish with clingfilm and leave to marinate in the refrigerator for at least 6 hours.

3 Preheat the barbecue. Drain the ribs, reserving the marinade. Cook over medium hot coals, turning and brushing frequently with the reserved marinade, for 30–40 minutes. Transfer to a large serving dish, garnish with the shredded spring onions and serve immediately.

lemon & herb pork escalopes

serves 4 **prep: 10 mins, plus 8 hrs** ⏲ **cook: 15 mins** ⏲
30 mins cooling/marinating

Although it is always important that pork is well done, be careful not to overcook these delicately flavoured, thin escalopes and be sure to grill them only on a medium barbecue.

INGREDIENTS

4 pork escalopes

2 tbsp sunflower oil

6 bay leaves, torn into pieces

grated rind and juice of 2 lemons

125 ml/4 fl oz beer

1 tbsp clear honey

6 juniper berries, lightly crushed

salt and pepper

1 crisp dessert apple

fresh flat-leaved parsley sprigs,

to garnish

NUTRITIONAL INFORMATION	
Calories	.349
Protein	.37g
Carbohydrate	.9g
Sugars	.9g
Fat	.18g
Saturates	.5g

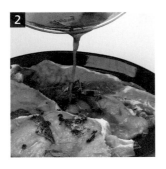

cook's tip

Turkey breast steaks would also be very tasty cooked in this way, but should be grilled for 7–8 minutes on each side. Make sure they are thoroughly cooked before serving.

1 Place the pork escalopes in a large, shallow, non-metallic dish. Heat the oil in a small, heavy-based saucepan. Add the bay leaves and stir-fry for 1 minute. Stir in the lemon rind and juice, beer, honey and juniper berries and season to taste with salt and pepper.

2 Pour the mixture over the pork, turning to coat. Cover with clingfilm, leave to cool, then leave to marinate in the refrigerator for up to 8 hours.

3 Preheat the barbecue. Drain the pork, reserving the marinade. Core the apple and cut into rings. Cook the pork over medium hot coals, brushing frequently with the reserved marinade, for 5 minutes on each side, or until thoroughly cooked. Cook the apples on the barbecue, brushing frequently with the marinade, for 3 minutes. Transfer the pork to a large serving plate with the apple rings, garnish with parsley sprigs and serve immediately.

gin & juniper pork

cook: 14–18 mins

prep: 10 mins, plus 8 hrs marinating

serves 4

This dish was originally cooked with wild boar, which is now being farmed and is available in some major supermarkets. It is equally delicious when made with pork chops.

NUTRITIONAL INFORMATION	
Calories	.425
Protein	.32g
Carbohydrate	.10g
Sugars	.8g
Fat	.26g
Saturates	.9g

INGREDIENTS

4 pork chops, about 175 g/6 oz each

50 ml/2 fl oz dry gin

175 ml/6 fl oz orange juice

2 red or white onions, cut in half

6 juniper berries, lightly crushed

thinly pared rind of 1 orange

1 cinnamon stick

1 bay leaf

2 tsp finely chopped fresh thyme

salt and pepper

cook's tip

Both red and white onions have a sweeter, milder flavour than brown onions, which is emphasised by chargrilling. Spanish onions are also mild, but as they are large, use only 1 and cut it into quarters.

1 Place the pork chops in a large, shallow, non-metallic dish. Pour in the gin and orange juice and add the onion halves. Add the juniper berries, orange rind, cinnamon stick, bay leaf and thyme and, using a fork, stir well until the pork chops are thoroughly coated. Cover with clingfilm and leave to marinate in the refrigerator for up to 8 hours.

2 Preheat the barbecue. Drain the pork chops and onions, reserving the marinade. Season the pork chops to taste with salt and pepper and sieve the marinade into a small jug.

3 Cook the pork and onions over medium hot coals, brushing frequently with the reserved marinade, for 7–9 minutes on each side, or until thoroughly cooked. Transfer to a large serving plate and serve immediately.

meatballs on sticks

serves 8 **prep: 20 mins** ⟲ **cook: 10 mins** ⟳

These are popular with children and adults alike. Serve with a selection of ready-made or home-made sauces, such as a Tomato Relish (see page 94), heated on the side of the barbecue.

INGREDIENTS

4 pork and herb sausages

115 g/4 oz fresh beef mince

85 g/3 oz fresh white breadcrumbs

1 onion, finely chopped

2 tbsp chopped mixed fresh herbs, such
as parsley, thyme and sage

1 egg

salt and pepper

sunflower oil, for brushing

sauces of your choice, to serve

NUTRITIONAL INFORMATION

Calories 132

Protein 9g

Carbohydrate 8g

Sugars 2g

Fat 7g

Saturates 3g

---

variation

Substitute 1 cooked potato and 1 cooked small beetroot, both finely chopped, for the breadcrumbs.

---

cook's tip

An increasing number of flavoured sausages are available, from leek and black pepper to chilli, and can be used for these meatballs.

1 Preheat the barbecue. Remove the sausage meat from the skins, place in a large bowl and break up with a fork. Add the beef mince, breadcrumbs, onion, herbs and egg. Season to taste with salt and pepper and stir well with a wooden spoon until thoroughly mixed.

2 Form the mixture into small balls, about the size of a golf ball, between the palms of your hands. Spear each one with a cocktail stick and brush with oil.

3 Cook over medium hot coals, turning frequently and brushing with more oil as necessary, for 10 minutes, or until cooked through. Transfer to a large serving plate and serve immediately with a choice of sauces.

bacon koftas

serves 4   **prep: 15 mins** ⏱   **cook: 10 mins** ⏱

Kofta – moulded kebabs – are usually made from a spicy mixture of minced lamb. These are economically based on lean bacon. While they are very easy to make, be careful not to over-process them.

INGREDIENTS

1 small onion

225 g/8 oz lean bacon, rinded and roughly chopped

85 g/3 oz fresh white breadcrumbs

1 tbsp chopped fresh marjoram

grated rind of 1 lemon

1 egg white

pepper

chopped nuts, for coating (optional)

paprika, to dust

snipped fresh chives to garnish

NUTRITIONAL INFORMATION	
Calories	180
Protein	12g
Carbohydrate	12g
Sugars	1g
Fat	10g
Saturates	4g

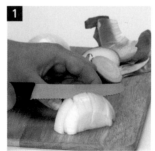

cook's tip

Be careful not to process the kofta mixture for too long. If it becomes too smooth, the koftas will be too sticky to shape, and will lose their delicious texture.

1 Preheat the barbecue, Using a sharp knife, chop the onion, then put it into a food processor with the bacon, breadcrumbs, marjoram, lemon rind and egg white. Season to taste with pepper and process briefly, just until the mixture is blended.

2 Divide the bacon mixture into 8 equal portions and form each around a skewer into a fat sausage. Dust the skewered koftas with paprika. If you like, form 4 of the portions into rounds rather than sausages, then spread the chopped nuts out on a large, flat plate and roll the rounds in them to coat.

3 Cook over hot coals for 10 minutes, turning frequently. Transfer to a large serving plate and serve immediately, garnished with snipped fresh chives.

pigs in blankets

cook: 15–20 mins **prep: 15 mins** serves 4

Sausages are traditional fare for the barbecue, but even speciality varieties can a be a little boring. Pigs in blankets, on the other hand, are always fun and delicious.

NUTRITIONAL INFORMATION	
Calories	.499
Protein	.31g
Carbohydrate	.6g
Sugars	.2g
Fat	.39g
Saturates	.16g

INGREDIENTS

115 g/4 oz mozzarella cheese

8 Toulouse sausages

2 tbsp Dijon mustard

8 smoked bacon rashers

cook's tip

Toulouse sausages are fairly large cooking sausages made from roughly chopped pork. They are widely available, but you can substitute other good-quality cooking sausages.

1 Preheat the barbecue. Thinly slice the mozzarella cheese. Cut a deep slit in the side of each sausage, using a sharp knife. Spread the cut sides with the mustard. Divide the slices of cheese between the sausages and reshape them.

2 Stretch the bacon with a heavy, flat-bladed knife. Wrap 1 bacon rasher tightly around each sausage to hold it together. If necessary, secure with a cocktail stick.

3 Cook over hot coals, turning frequently, for 15–20 minutes. Transfer to a large serving plate and serve immediately.

easy mixed grill

⏱ **cook: 12 mins**　　　　⏱ **prep: 20 mins**　　　　**serves 4**

NUTRITIONAL INFORMATION

Calories	1083
Protein	. . . . .42g
Carbohydrate	. . . . .28g
Sugars	. . . . .23g
Fat	. . . . .90g
Saturates	. . . . .23g

variation

If you like, substitute medallions or noisettes of other meats, such as lamb or chicken, for the steak.

A meat feast, this mixed grill includes everything a red-blooded carnivore could want – sausages, bacon, steak and kidney. Ideal served with baked potatoes and a crisp green salad.

INGREDIENTS

4 lambs' kidneys	12 bay leaves
6 smoked back bacon rashers, rinded	salt and pepper
4 cherry tomatoes	1 quantity Spicy Marinade
4 small fillet steaks or tournedos	(see page 105)
8 small pork sausages	Mustard Butter (see page 112),
4 button mushrooms	to serve

cook's tip

For even cooking, try to ensure that all the pieces of meat are about the same size and make sure that the skewers are not overcrowded, otherwise the meat may not cook properly.

1 Preheat the barbecue. Using a sharp knife, trim the kidneys, cut in half and, using a pair of kitchen scissors, remove the cores. Cut the bacon rashers in half across the centre, then wrap a piece of bacon around each kidney half and around each cherry tomato.

2 Thread the kidneys, tomatoes, steaks, sausages, mushrooms and bay leaves alternately on to metal skewers. Season to taste with salt and pepper and brush with the marinade.

3 Cook over medium hot coals, turning and brushing frequently with the marinade, for 12 minutes.

Transfer to a large serving plate and serve immediately with the Mustard Butter.

frankly fabulous skewers

serves 4   **prep: 10 mins** ⟲   **cook: 40 mins** ⟳

A new way with an old favourite – cook frankfurter sausages on the barbecue for a wonderful smoky flavour and an incredibly easy meal. They are served here with garlic toast.

INGREDIENTS

12 frankfurter sausages

2 courgettes, cut into 1-cm/½-inch slices

2 corn cobs, cut into 1-cm/½-inch slices

12 cherry tomatoes

12 baby onions

2 tbsp olive oil

GARLIC TOAST

2 garlic bulbs

2–3 tbsp olive oil

1 baguette, sliced

salt and pepper

NUTRITIONAL INFORMATION

Calories 620

Protein 19g

Carbohydrate 69g

Sugars 6g

Fat 32g

Saturates 2g

variation

Slice a baguette without cutting it right through. Spread with 2 crushed garlic cloves beaten into 115 g/4 oz butter. Wrap in foil and cook for 15 minutes.

cook's tip

When toasting the baguette, do not put the bread directly over very hot coals. Keep a close watch on them as they only take a few minutes to cook and will burn easily.

1 Preheat the barbecue. To make the garlic toast, slice off the tops of the garlic bulbs. Brush the bulbs with oil and wrap them in foil. Cook over hot coals, turning occasionally, for 30 minutes.

2 Meanwhile, cut each frankfurter sausage into 3 pieces. Thread the frankfurter pieces, courgette slices, corn cob slices, cherry tomatoes and baby onions alternately on to metal skewers. Brush with olive oil.

3 Cook the skewers over hot coals, turning and brushing frequently with the oil, for 8–10 minutes. Meanwhile, brush the slices of baguette with oil and toast both sides on the barbecue.

Unwrap the garlic bulbs and squeeze the cloves on to the bread. Season to taste with salt and pepper and drizzle over a little extra olive oil, if you like. Transfer the skewers to a large serving plate and serve immediately with the garlic toast.

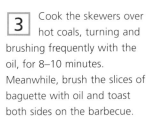

vegetables

The range of vegetables that can be cooked on the barbecue is immense and some, such as courgettes, aubergines, red onions and peppers, seem almost designed for the purpose. As they grill, they acquire a delicious sweetness and they look appetisingly attractive.

Some of the recipes in this chapter, for example Greek Vegetable Kebabs (see page 128), Mushroom Burgers (see page 139) and Summer Vegetable Parcels (see page 144), can be served as a vegetarian main course, and a number are also suitable for vegans. Other recipes, such as Potato Fans (see page 133), are designed as accompaniments to fish, poultry, meat or vegetarian dishes. Still others, like Cajun Vegetables (see page 147), can serve either purpose if you adjust the quantities accordingly. Finally, you can serve many of these dishes, such as Stuffed Tomato Parcels (see page 132) and Aubergines with Tsatziki (see page 153), as starters while you are cooking the main course.

No barbecue would be complete without at least one salad and a selection is even better. A mixed leaf salad is simplicity itself – you can even buy them ready made, complete with a dressing – and you could complement this with one of the four at the end of this chapter. Rice- and pasta-based salads are substantial and popular, and if you are entertaining, impress your guests with the fashionable Lebanese Tabbouleh (see page 156) or the flamboyant Red & Green Salad (see page 159).

greek vegetable kebabs

cook: 35 mins

**prep: 20 mins, plus
40 mins cooling**

serves 4

NUTRITIONAL INFORMATION	
Calories	.428
Protein	.19g
Carbohydrate	.40g
Sugars	.21g
Fat	.23g
Saturates	.4g

*A complete meal on a skewer, these tasty kebabs include
a selection of vegetables, cheese and, perhaps surprisingly,
nectarines, in an extremely colourful combination.*

INGREDIENTS

2 onions

8 new potatoes, washed
but not peeled

salt

1 aubergine, cut into 8 pieces

8 thick slices cucumber

1 red pepper, deseeded and cut
into 8 pieces

1 yellow pepper, deseeded and cut
into 8 pieces

225 g/8 oz halloumi cheese,
cut into 8 cubes

2 nectarines, stoned and quartered

8 button mushrooms

2 tbsp olive oil

2 tsp chopped fresh thyme

2 tsp chopped fresh rosemary

1 quantity Tsatziki (see page 153),
to serve

variation

Although not authentically Greek, you
could serve these kebabs with Aïoli
(see page 41). You can substitute feta
for the halloumi cheese, if you like.

cook's tip

Halloumi, a ewe's milk cheese,
is perfect for barbecues
because it softens and chars
without melting. Keep a close
watch on it as it may burn.

1 Preheat the barbecue.
Cut the onions into
wedges, then place the onions
and potatoes in a saucepan of
lightly salted boiling water and
cook for 20 minutes, or until
just tender. Drain and leave to
cool. Meanwhile, blanch the
aubergine in boiling water
for 2 minutes, then add the
cucumber and simmer for
1 minute. Add the peppers

and simmer for a further
2 minutes, then drain and
leave the vegetables to cool.

2 Place the cooled
vegetables, cheese,
nectarines and mushrooms in
a bowl. Add the olive oil and
herbs and toss to coat. Thread
the vegetables, cheese,
nectarines and mushrooms on
to several metal skewers.

3 Cook the kebabs over
hot coals, turning
frequently, for 15 minutes.
Transfer to a large serving
plate and serve immediately
with the Tsatziki.

chargrilled vegetables with creamy pesto

serves 4 **prep: 30 mins** **cook: 8 mins**

Vegetables, especially baby varieties, taste wonderful when cooked on the barbecue. Here they are served with a delicious pesto, which complements them perfectly. Serve with grilled meat.

INGREDIENTS

1 red onion	**CREAMY PESTO**
1 fennel bulb	55 g/2 oz fresh basil leaves
4 baby aubergines	15 g/½ oz pine kernels
4 baby courgettes	1 garlic clove
1 orange pepper	pinch of coarse sea salt
1 red pepper	25 g/1 oz freshly grated
2 beef tomatoes	Parmesan cheese
2 tbsp olive oil	50 ml/2 fl oz extra virgin olive oil
salt and pepper	150 ml/5 fl oz natural Greek yogurt
	1 fresh basil sprig, to garnish

NUTRITIONAL INFORMATION

Calories	.313
Protein	.10g
Carbohydrate	.15g
Sugars	.11g
Fat	.24g
Saturates	.6g

variation

If baby vegetables are not available, you can cut 2 aubergines into slices and cut 2 courgettes in half lengthways instead.

cook's tip

This home-made pesto mixture, without the added yogurt, will keep in a screw-top jar in the refrigerator for up to 3 days. If it seems to be drying out, pour a layer of olive oil over the top.

1 Preheat the barbecue. To make the creamy pesto, place the basil, pine kernels, garlic and sea salt in a mortar and pound to a paste with a pestle. Gradually work in the Parmesan cheese, then gradually stir in the oil. Place the yogurt in a small serving bowl and stir in 3–4 tablespoons of the pesto mixture. Cover with clingfilm

and leave to chill in the refrigerator until required. Store any leftover pesto mixture in a screw-top jar in the refrigerator.

2 Prepare the vegetables. Cut the onion and fennel bulb into wedges, trim the aubergines and courgettes, deseed and halve the peppers and cut the tomatoes in half.

Brush the vegetables with oil and season to taste with salt and pepper.

3 Cook the aubergines and peppers over hot coals for 3 minutes, then add the courgettes, onion and tomatoes and cook, turning occasionally and brushing with more oil if necessary, for a further 5 minutes. Transfer to

a large serving plate and serve immediately with the pesto, garnished with a basil sprig.

stuffed tomato parcels

serves 4　　　**prep: 15 mins, plus 15 mins cooling**　　　**cook: 20 mins**

An unusual filling for stuffed tomatoes, the spinach and cheese are given extra flavour with toasted sunflower seeds.

INGREDIENTS

1 tbsp olive oil

2 tbsp sunflower seeds

1 onion, finely chopped

1 garlic clove, finely chopped

500 g/1 lb 2 oz fresh spinach, thick stalks removed and leaves shredded

pinch of freshly grated nutmeg

salt and pepper

4 beef tomatoes

140 g/5 oz mozzarella cheese, diced

NUTRITIONAL INFORMATION	
Calories	.248
Protein	.16g
Carbohydrate	.11g
Sugars	.9g
Fat	.16g
Saturates	.6g

cook's tip

Dry-roasting sunflower seeds brings out their delicate nutty flavour, but keep stirring constantly as they will burn very easily.

1 Preheat the barbecue. Heat the oil in a heavy-based saucepan. Add the sunflower seeds and cook, stirring constantly, for 2 minutes, or until golden. Add the onion and cook over a low heat, stirring occasionally, for 5 minutes, or until softened but not browned. Add the garlic and spinach, cover and cook for

2–3 minutes, or until the spinach has wilted. Remove the saucepan from the heat and season to taste with nutmeg, salt and pepper. Leave to cool.

2 Using a sharp knife, cut off and reserve a thin slice from the top of each tomato and scoop out the flesh with a teaspoon, taking

care not to pierce the shell. Chop the flesh and stir it into the spinach mixture with the mozzarella cheese.

3 Fill the tomato shells with the spinach and cheese mixture and replace the tops. Cut 4 squares of foil, each large enough to enclose a tomato. Place one tomato in the centre of each square and

fold up the sides to enclose securely. Cook over hot coals, turning occasionally, for 10 minutes. Serve immediately in the parcels.

potato fans

⏱ **cook: 1 hr**   ◷ **prep: 5 mins**   **serves 6**

These garlic-flavoured roast potatoes make a wonderful alternative to baked potatoes. Allow plenty of time for cooking.

NUTRITIONAL INFORMATION	
Calories	235
Protein	. . . . .6g
Carbohydrate	. . . . .46g
Sugars	. . . . .2g
Fat	. . . . .4g
Saturates	. . . . .1g

INGREDIENTS

6 large potatoes, scrubbed but
not peeled
2 tbsp garlic-flavoured olive oil

cook's tip

If you do not have any garlic-flavoured oil, pour 2 tablespoons olive oil into a bowl, add 1 crushed garlic clove, cover with clingfilm and leave to infuse for 2 hours, then use as above.

1 Preheat the barbecue. Using a sharp knife, make a series of cuts across the potatoes almost all the way through. Cut out 6 squares of foil, each large enough to enclose a potato.

2 Place a potato on each square of foil and brush generously with the garlic-flavoured oil. Fold up the sides of the foil to enclose the potatoes completely.

3 Cook over hot coals, turning occasionally, for 1 hour. To serve, open the foil parcels and gently pinch the potatoes to open up the fans.

spicy caribbean kebabs

serves 4   **prep: 20 mins, plus 3 hrs marinating**   **cook: 15 mins**

Bring a taste of the tropics to your barbecue with these sizzling vegetable kebabs. They make a delicious vegetarian main course and are also suitable for vegans.

INGREDIENTS

1 corn cob

1 christophene, peeled and cut into chunks

1 ripe plantain, peeled and cut into thick slices

1 aubergine, cut into chunks

1 red pepper, deseeded and cut into chunks

1 green pepper, deseeded and cut into chunks

1 onion, cut into wedges

8 button mushrooms

4 cherry tomatoes

MARINADE

150 ml/5 fl oz tomato juice

4 tbsp sunflower oil

4 tbsp lime juice

3 tbsp dark soy sauce

1 shallot, finely chopped

2 garlic cloves, finely chopped

1 fresh green chilli, deseeded and finely chopped

½ tsp ground cinnamon

pepper

NUTRITIONAL INFORMATION

Calories 250

Protein 5g

Carbohydrate 31g

Sugars 13g

Fat 13g

Saturates 2g

---

variation

If you prefer, replace the green pepper with a sweeter orange or red pepper and the aubergine with 1 courgette, cut into chunks.

cook's tip

Christophene, also known as chayote, is a pear-shaped gourd widely used in Caribbean cooking because it readily absorbs spicy flavours. If you cannot find it, use pumpkin or courgettes instead.

---

1 Using a sharp knife, remove the husks and silks from the corn cob and cut into 2.5-cm/1-inch thick slices. Blanch the christophene chunks in boiling water for 2 minutes. Drain, refresh under cold running water and drain again. Place the christophene chunks in a large bowl with the corn cob slices and the remaining ingredients.

2 Mix all the marinade ingredients together in a jug, seasoning to taste with pepper. Pour the marinade over the vegetables, tossing to coat. Cover with clingfilm and leave to marinate in the refrigerator for 3 hours.

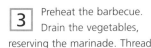

3 Preheat the barbecue. Drain the vegetables, reserving the marinade. Thread the vegetables on to several metal skewers. Cook over hot coals, turning and brushing frequently with the reserved marinade, for 10–15 minutes. Transfer to a large serving plate and serve immediately.

courgette & cheese parcels

cook: 30 mins   **prep: 10 mins**   serves 4

NUTRITIONAL INFORMATION

Calories 172

Protein 9g

Carbohydrate 8g

Sugars 6g

Fat 12g

Saturates 1g

variation

If you like, substitute mozzarella cheese or fontina for the feta cheese and replace the mint with the same amount of fresh parsley.

These delicately flavoured, melt-in-the-mouth stuffed courgettes are ideal if you are serving food to both meat-eaters and vegetarians, as the parcels can be cooked in the barbecue embers and so avoid any contact with meat on the grill.

INGREDIENTS

1 small bunch of fresh mint

8 courgettes

1 tbsp olive oil, plus extra for brushing

115 g/4 oz feta cheese, cut into strips

pepper

cook's tip

Use long-handled tongs to place the parcels on to the barbecue embers and to remove them when done. Be careful when opening the parcels as they will be extremely hot.

1 Preheat the barbecue. Using a sharp knife, finely chop enough mint to fill 1 tablespoon. Reserve until required. Cut out 8 rectangles of foil, each large enough to enclose a courgette, and brush lightly with olive oil. Cut a slit along the length of each courgette and place them on the foil rectangles.

2 Insert strips of feta cheese along the slits in the courgettes, then drizzle the olive oil over the top, sprinkle with the reserved chopped mint and season to taste with pepper. Fold in the sides of the foil rectangles securely and seal the edges to enclose the cheese-stuffed courgettes completely.

3 Bake the courgette parcels in the barbecue embers for 30 minutes. Carefully unwrap the parcels and serve immediately.

cheese & red onion kebabs

serves 4　　　　**prep: 10 mins, plus 2 hrs marinating**　　　　**cook: 10–15 mins**

Red onions have a mild, sweet flavour and retain their attractive colour when cooked. Here, they are barbecued with apples and salty cheese for a wonderful combination of flavours and textures.

INGREDIENTS

3 red onions

450 g/1 lb halloumi cheese, cut into 2.5-cm/1-inch cubes

2 tart eating apples, cored and cut into wedges

4 tbsp olive oil

1 tbsp cider vinegar

1 tbsp Dijon mustard

1 garlic clove, finely chopped

1 tsp finely chopped sage

salt and pepper

NUTRITIONAL INFORMATION

Calories	.449
Protein	.21g
Carbohydrate	.16g
Sugars	.13g
Fat	.34g
Saturates	.2g

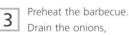

variation

If you like, you could serve these kebabs with Mild Mustard Sauce (see page 13) or even Sweet & Sour Relish (see page 87).

1 Cut the onions into wedges, then place in a large, shallow, non-metallic dish with the cheese and apples. Mix the oil, vinegar, mustard, garlic and sage together in a jug and season to taste with salt and pepper.

2 Pour the marinade over the onions, cheese and apples, tossing to coat. Cover with clingfilm and leave to marinate in the refrigerator for 2 hours.

3 Preheat the barbecue. Drain the onions, cheese and apples, reserving the marinade. Thread the onions, cheese and apples alternately on to several metal skewers. Cook over hot coals, turning and brushing frequently with the reserved marinade, for 10–15 minutes. Transfer to a large serving plate and serve immediately.

mushroom burgers

cook: 20 mins

prep: 25 mins, plus
1 hr chilling

serves 4

*Like their meaty cousins, home-made veggie burgers taste
much more flavoursome – and are usually a good deal healthier –
than the shop-bought varieties.*

NUTRITIONAL INFORMATION	
Calories	164
Protein	7g
Carbohydrate	24g
Sugars	4g
Fat	5g
Saturates	1g

INGREDIENTS

115 g/4 oz mushrooms

2 tsp sunflower oil, plus extra
for brushing

1 carrot

1 onion

1 courgette

25 g/1 oz peanuts

115 g/4 oz fresh white breadcrumbs

1 tbsp chopped fresh parsley

1 tsp yeast extract

salt and pepper

1 tbsp plain flour, for dusting

 Using a sharp knife, finely chop the mushrooms, then chop the carrot, onion and courgette and reserve. Heat the oil in a heavy-based frying pan, add the mushrooms and cook, stirring, for 8 minutes, or until all the moisture has evaporated. Using a slotted spoon, transfer the cooked mushrooms to a large bowl.

2 Put the carrot, onion, courgette and peanuts into a food processor and process until finely chopped. Transfer to the bowl and stir in the breadcrumbs, chopped parsley and yeast extract. Season to taste with salt and pepper. Lightly flour your hands and form the mixture into 4 patties. Place on a large plate, cover with clingfilm and leave to chill in the refrigerator for at least 1 hour and up to 1 day.

3 Preheat the barbecue. Brush the mushroom burgers with the sunflower oil and cook over hot coals for 8–10 minutes. Serve.

variation

Other nuts could also be used to make the burgers. Try cashew nuts, hazelnuts, or even a mixture of hazelnuts and pistachios.

vegetarian brochettes

cook: 8–10 mins   **prep: 20 mins**   **serves 4**

NUTRITIONAL INFORMATION

Calories 174

Protein 10g

Carbohydrate 11g

Sugars 8g

Fat 10g

Saturates 3g

variation

You can also make just vegetable brochettes. Omit the tofu and use aubergine chunks, courgette chunks and small strips of red pepper.

The great thing about tofu – apart from the fact that it is packed with protein – is its ability to absorb other flavours, in this case a mustard and honey flavoured glaze.

INGREDIENTS

2 courgettes

1 yellow pepper, deseeded and quartered

225 g/8 oz firm tofu (drained weight)

4 cherry tomatoes

4 baby onions

8 button mushrooms

HONEY GLAZE

2 tbsp olive oil

1 tbsp Meaux mustard

1 tbsp clear honey

salt and pepper

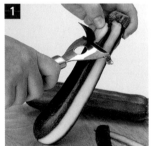

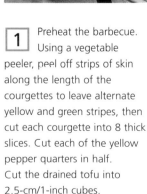

cook's tip

Meaux mustard is made from crushed black mustard seeds and vinegar. It is usually quite hot and is available from most large supermarkets. If you cannot find it, use Dijon mustard instead.

1 Preheat the barbecue. Using a vegetable peeler, peel off strips of skin along the length of the courgettes to leave alternate yellow and green stripes, then cut each courgette into 8 thick slices. Cut each of the yellow pepper quarters in half. Cut the drained tofu into 2.5-cm/1-inch cubes.

2 Thread the pieces of pepper, courgette slices, tofu cubes, cherry tomatoes, baby onions and button mushrooms on to 4 metal skewers. To make the glaze, mix the olive oil, mustard and honey together in a jug and season to taste with salt and pepper.

3 Brush the brochettes with the honey glaze and cook over medium hot coals, turning and brushing frequently with the glaze, for 8–10 minutes. Serve.

vegetable platter

serves 4 **prep: 25 mins, plus 1 hr marinating** **cook: 30 mins**

This cornucopia of chargrilled vegetables makes a wonderful vegetarian barbecue. Equally, the vegetables can be served as accompaniments to meat or fish.

INGREDIENTS

2 red onions	1 green pepper
2 white onions	1 yellow pepper
2 fennel bulbs	1 orange pepper
6 baby corn cobs	1 red pepper
12 cherry tomatoes	1 tbsp sunflower oil
4 tbsp olive oil	Lemon Mayonnaise (see page 13),
1 tbsp lemon juice	to serve
3 garlic cloves, finely chopped	
2 tbsp chopped fresh marjoram	
salt and pepper	

NUTRITIONAL INFORMATION

Calories 194

Protein 4g

Carbohydrate 13g

Sugars 10g

Fat 15g

Saturates 2g

variation

If you prefer, replace the Lemon Mayonnaise with plain Mayonnaise (see page 13) or try Creamy Pesto (see page 130) instead.

cook's tip

When marinating vegetables, it is not necessary to keep them in the refrigerator. You can leave them in a cool place, covered with clingfilm.

1 Using a sharp knife, cut the red and white onions in half and reserve until required. Blanch the fennel and corn cobs in a large saucepan of boiling water for 2 minutes. Drain, refresh under cold running water and drain again. Cut the fennel bulbs in half and place in a large, shallow, non-metallic dish. Cut the corn cobs in half across the centre and add to the dish with the tomatoes and onions.

2 Mix the oil, lemon juice, garlic and marjoram in a jug and season to taste with salt and pepper. Pour the mixture over the vegetables, cover with clingfilm and leave to marinate for 1 hour.

3 Preheat the barbecue. Drain the vegetables, reserving the marinade. Thread the corn and cherry tomatoes alternately on to presoaked wooden skewers. Brush the peppers with oil and cook over medium hot coals, turning frequently, for 10 minutes. Add the onion and fennel to the barbecue and cook, brushing with the marinade, for 5 minutes. Turn the onion and fennel and brush with marinade. Add the skewers, brush with marinade and cook, turning and brushing frequently with more marinade, for 10 minutes. Transfer the vegetables to a large plate and serve with the Lemon Mayonnaise.

summer vegetable parcels

cook: 25–30 mins **prep: 15 mins** **serves 4**

variation

If baby vegetables are unavailable, then use larger vegetables cut into small pieces, such as courgette and carrot batons and aubergine chunks.

You can use any baby vegetables you like – patty pan squash, corn cobs and plum tomatoes look attractive and add colour. Serve with grilled meat or fish for a substantial barbecue main course.

INGREDIENTS

1 kg/2 lb 4 oz mixed baby vegetables, such as carrots, patty pan squash, corn cobs, plum tomatoes, leeks, courgettes and onions

1 lemon

115 g/4 oz unsalted butter

3 tbsp chopped mixed fresh herbs, such as parsley, thyme and chervil

2 garlic cloves

salt and pepper

cook's tip

It is best to use a double thickness of foil to make parcels for cooking on the barbecue so that they don't tear when you turn them.

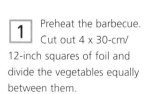

1 Preheat the barbecue. Cut out 4 x 30-cm/ 12-inch squares of foil and divide the vegetables equally between them.

2 Using a grater, finely grate the lemon rind, then squeeze the juice from the lemon and reserve until required. Put the lemon rind, butter, herbs and garlic into a

food processor and process until blended, then season to taste with salt and pepper. Alternatively, beat together in a bowl until blended.

3 Divide the butter equally between the vegetables, dotting it on top. Fold up the sides of the foil to enclose the vegetables, sealing securely. Cook over medium

hot coals, turning occasionally, for 25–30 minutes. Open the parcels, sprinkle with the reserved lemon juice and serve immediately.

corn-on-the-cob with blue cheese dressing

serves 6   **prep: 15 mins** ⏱   **cook: 15–20 mins** ⏱

Corn cobs are delicious grilled on the barbecue. Cook them as soon after purchase as possible because they quickly lose their sweetness as their natural sugars convert to starch.

INGREDIENTS

140 g/5 oz Danish Blue cheese

140 g/5 oz curd cheese

125 ml/4 fl oz natural Greek yogurt

salt and pepper

6 corn cobs in their husks

NUTRITIONAL INFORMATION	
Calories 255	
Protein 12g	
Carbohydrate 21g	
Sugars 4g	
Fat 14g	
Saturates 8g	

cook's tip

When buying corn cobs, always make sure that they are as fresh as possible and only choose ones that have golden tassels and are heavy.

1 Preheat the barbecue. Crumble the Danish Blue cheese, then place in a bowl. Beat with a wooden spoon until creamy. Beat in the curd cheese until thoroughly blended. Gradually beat in the yogurt and season to taste with salt and pepper. Cover with clingfilm and leave to chill in the refrigerator until required.

2 Fold back the husks on each corn cob and remove the silks. Smooth the husks back into place. Cut out 6 rectangles of foil, each large enough to enclose a corn cob. Wrap the corn cobs in the foil.

3 Cook the corn cobs over hot coals, turning frequently, for 15–20 minutes. Unwrap the corn cobs and discard the foil. Peel back the husk on one side of each and trim off with a sharp knife or kitchen scissors. Serve immediately with the blue cheese dressing.

cajun vegetables

cook: 12–15 mins   **prep: 10 mins**   serves 4

These spicy vegetables would be a perfect accompaniment to Blackened Chicken (see page 71) and would also go well with Caribbean Sea Bass (see page 20).

NUTRITIONAL INFORMATION	
Calories	.244
Protein	.5g
Carbohydrate	.41g
Sugars	.8g
Fat	.8g
Saturates	.4g

INGREDIENTS

4 corn cobs

2 sweet potatoes

25 g/1 oz butter, melted

SPICE MIX

2 teaspoons paprika

1 teaspoon ground cumin

1 teaspoon ground coriander

1 teaspoon ground black pepper

½–1 teaspoon chilli powder

cook's tip

The flesh of sweet potatoes varies in colour from white to orange. Not only are the orange-fleshed varieties more attractive, they also contain more nutrients.

1 Preheat the barbecue. To make the spice mix, mix all the ingredients together in a small bowl.

2 Remove the husks and silks from the corn cobs, then cut each cob into 4 equal chunks. Cut the sweet potatoes into thick slices, but do not peel. Brush the corn chunks and sweet potato slices with melted butter and sprinkle with some spice mix.

3 Cook the corn cobs and sweet potatoes over medium hot coals, turning frequently, for 12–15 minutes. Brush with more melted butter and sprinkle with extra spice mixture during cooking.

Transfer the corn and sweet potatoes to a large serving plate and serve immediately.

aubergine & sweet potato rolls

serves 4–6 **prep: 30 mins** ⏲ **cook: 45–50 mins** ⏲

*Partially cooked in advance, these attractive little rolls with a
tasty filling are baked in foil parcels.*

INGREDIENTS

450 g/1 lb sweet potatoes

salt and black pepper

4 spring onions, chopped

175 g/6 oz Gruyère cheese, diced

1 red pepper, deseeded and chopped

1 garlic clove, crushed

1 tsp chopped fresh thyme

25 g/1 oz plain flour

1½ tsp paprika

1½ tsp curry powder

1½ tsp celery salt

1 tsp caster sugar

1 tbsp garlic granules

4 large aubergines

3 tbsp olive oil, plus extra

for brushing

NUTRITIONAL INFORMATION

Calories 452

Protein 17g

Carbohydrate 39g

Sugars 16g

Fat 27g

Saturates 11g

---

variation

Emmenthal cheese would also work
well in this dish. If you like, substitute
the same quantity of Emmenthal
cheese for the Gruyère cheese.

---

cook's tip

Salting aubergine slices will
prevent them from soaking up
too much oil during frying.
Place in a colander, sprinkle the
flesh with salt and stand for
30 minutes. Rinse and pat dry.

1 Preheat the barbecue. Cook the sweet potatoes in a saucepan of boiling salted water for 20 minutes, or until tender. Drain and leave until cool enough to handle. Peel and mash in a large bowl until smooth. Add the spring onions, cheese, red pepper, garlic and thyme and season to taste with salt and pepper.

2 Place the flour on a large plate and stir in the paprika, curry powder, celery salt, sugar and garlic granules. Slice each aubergine lengthways into quarters and dust with the seasoned flour. Heat half the olive oil in a large, heavy-based frying pan. Add the aubergine slices, in batches, and cook until just golden brown, adding more oil as necessary. Remove with a slotted spoon and leave to cool.

3 Place a spoonful of the sweet potato mixture on each aubergine slice and roll up. Cut out 4 x 30-cm/ 12-inch squares of foil and brush with oil. Place 4 aubergine rolls on each square and fold up the sides to enclose the rolls. Cook over medium hot coals, turning occasionally, for 25–30 minutes. Unwrap the parcels and transfer the rolls to a large serving dish. Serve immediately.

indian kebabs

cook: 10–12 mins   **prep: 15 mins**   **serves 4**

variation

Replace the cauliflower florets with broccoli florets and the orange pepper with either red or green pepper.

Vegetables, fruit and cheese, brushed with a spicy glaze, need no more than a plate of salad to make a delicious vegetarian meal.

INGREDIENTS

175 g/6 oz paneer	GLAZE
8 cherry tomatoes	2 tbsp lime juice
1 orange pepper, deseeded and cut	2 tbsp chilli sauce
into pieces	1 tbsp vegetable oil
8 cauliflower florets	1 tbsp clear honey
3 pineapple slices, cut into quarters	1 tbsp water
1 mango, peeled, stoned and	pinch of ground cumin
cut into cubes	salt and pepper

cook's tip

Paneer is a soft Indian cheese made by curdling milk with lemon juice, before straining and pressing flat. It is available from Indian shops, but tofu could be used as a substitute.

1 Preheat the barbecue. Place all the ingredients for the glaze in a small bowl, seasoning to taste with salt and pepper. Using a balloon whisk, whisk until thoroughly blended. Reserve until required.

2 Using a sharp knife, cut the paneer into 2.5-cm/1-inch cubes. Thread the tomatoes, orange pepper pieces, cauliflower florets, pineapple pieces, mango cubes and paneer cubes on to 4 long metal skewers.

3 Brush the kebabs with the glaze and cook over medium hot coals, turning and brushing frequently with the glaze, for 10–12 minutes. Serve the kebabs immediately.

prune, apricot & onion skewers

serves 4   **prep: 15 mins** ⏲   **cook: 25 mins** ⏲

These flavoursome, fruity skewers would go well with plainly grilled pork chops, duck breasts, lamb steaks or kebabs, as they will counteract the richness of the meat.

INGREDIENTS

500 g/1 lb 2 oz baby onions

175 g/6 oz prunes, stoned

225 g/8 oz dried apricots, stoned

5-cm/2-inch cinnamon stick

225 ml/8 fl oz white wine

2 tbsp chilli sauce

2 tbsp sunflower oil

NUTRITIONAL INFORMATION

Calories 292

Protein 5g

Carbohydrate 48g

Sugars 45g

Fat 6g

Saturates 1g

cook's tip

Baby onions are also known as pearl onions and have a delicate sweet flavour. If you cannot find them, then use shallots or 1 white onion, cut into chunks.

1 Cut the tops off the onions and peel off the skin. Reserve until required. Place the prunes, apricots, cinnamon and wine in a heavy-based saucepan and bring to the boil. Reduce the heat and simmer for 5 minutes. Drain, reserving the cooking liquid, and leave the fruit until cool enough to handle.

2 Return the cooking liquid and cinnamon stick to the saucepan, return to the boil and boil until reduced by half. Remove the saucepan from the heat and remove and discard the cinnamon stick. Stir in the chilli sauce and oil.

3 Thread the prunes, apricots and onions on to several metal skewers. Cook over medium hot coals, turning and brushing frequently with the wine mixture, for 10 minutes. Serve immediately.

aubergines with tsatziki

 cook: 10 mins   prep: 15 minutes   serves 4

This makes a delicious starter for a barbecue party or can be served as part of a vegetarian barbecue meze with Stuffed Tomato Parcels (see page 132), or Courgette & Cheese Parcels (see page 136).

NUTRITIONAL INFORMATION	
Calories	137
Protein	5g
Carbohydrate	5g
Sugars	5g
Fat	11g
Saturates	4g

INGREDIENTS

2 tbsp olive oil

salt and pepper

2 aubergines, thinly sliced

TSATZIKI

½ cucumber

200 ml/7 fl oz natural Greek yogurt

4 spring onions, finely chopped

1 garlic clove, finely chopped

3 tbsp chopped fresh mint

salt and pepper

1 fresh mint sprig, to garnish

cook's tip

An alternative dip to serve with the aubergines can be made by blending 300 ml/ 10 fl oz soured cream with 2 crushed garlic cloves. Season and chill before serving.

1 Preheat the barbecue. To make the tsatziki, finely chop the cucumber. Place the yogurt in a bowl and beat well until smooth. Stir in the cucumber, spring onions, garlic and mint. Season to taste with salt and pepper. Transfer to a serving bowl, cover with clingfilm and leave to chill in the refrigerator until required.

2 Season the olive oil with salt and pepper, then brush the aubergine slices with the oil.

3 Cook the aubergines over hot coals for 5 minutes on each side, brushing with more oil, if necessary. Transfer to a large serving plate and serve immediately with the tsatziki, garnished with a mint sprig.

tropical rice salad

Rice salads are always popular and this colourful, fruity mixture goes especially well with barbecued meat or chicken.

INGREDIENTS

115 g/4 oz long-grain rice

salt and pepper

4 spring onions

225 g/8 oz canned pineapple pieces in natural juice

200 g/7 oz canned sweetcorn, drained

2 red peppers, deseeded and diced

3 tbsp sultanas

DRESSING

1 tbsp groundnut oil

1 tbsp hazelnut oil

1 tbsp light soy sauce

1 garlic clove, finely chopped

1 tsp chopped fresh root ginger

NUTRITIONAL INFORMATION

Calories 300

Protein 5g

Carbohydrate 57g

Sugars 26g

Fat 7g

Saturates 1g

variation

Try other flavoured nut oils, such as walnut oil or sesame oil. You can also substitute sunflower oil for the groundnut oil, if you like.

cook's tip

Before using long-grain rice, rinse it thoroughly under cold running water to remove any impurities. Once cooked, it is important to rinse it again to remove all the excess starch.

1 Cook the rice in a large saucepan of lightly salted boiling water for 15 minutes, or until tender. Drain thoroughly and rinse under cold running water. Place the rice in a large serving bowl.

2 Using a sharp knife, finely chop the spring onions. Drain the pineapple pieces, reserving the juice in a jug. Add the pineapple pieces, sweetcorn, red peppers, chopped spring onions and sultanas to the rice and mix lightly.

3 Add all the dressing ingredients to the reserved pineapple juice, whisking well, and season to taste with salt and pepper.

Pour the dressing over the salad and toss until the salad is thoroughly coated. Serve immediately.

tabbouleh

serves 4   prep: 10 mins, plus 1 hr 🕐
30 mins standing/marinating   cook: 0 mins 🕐

This Middle Eastern salad is increasingly fashionable. It is a classic accompaniment for lamb, but goes well with most grilled meat.

INGREDIENTS

175 g/6 oz bulgar wheat

3 tbsp extra virgin olive oil

4 tbsp lemon juice

salt and pepper

4 spring onions

1 green pepper, deseeded and sliced

4 tomatoes, chopped

2 tbsp chopped fresh parsley

2 tbsp chopped fresh mint

8 black olives, stoned

fresh mint sprigs, to garnish

NUTRITIONAL INFORMATION

Calories	.265
Protein	.6g
Carbohydrate	.37g
Sugars	.4g
Fat	.11g
Saturates	.2g

variation

Use different types of fresh tomatoes – try vine-ripened tomatoes, which have a delicate, sweet flavour, or cherry tomatoes, cut in half.

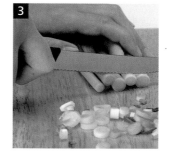

cook's tip

The grains of bulgar wheat have been cracked by boiling and so are partially cooked, so all it needs is rehydrating. Don't make this salad too far in advance as it may go soggy..

1 Place the bulgar wheat in a large bowl and add enough cold water to cover. Leave to stand for 30 minutes, or until the wheat has doubled in size. Drain well and press out as much liquid as possible. Spread out the wheat on kitchen paper to dry.

2 Place the wheat in a serving bowl. Mix the olive oil and lemon juice together in a jug and season to taste with salt and pepper. Pour the lemon mixture over the wheat and leave to marinate for 1 hour.

3 Using a sharp knife, finely chop the spring onions, then add to the salad with the green pepper, tomatoes, parsley and mint and toss lightly to mix. Top the salad with the olives and garnish with fresh mint sprigs, then serve.

cheese & walnut pasta salad

serves 4　　　　**prep: 15 mins** ⏲　　　　**cook: 10–15 mins** ⏲

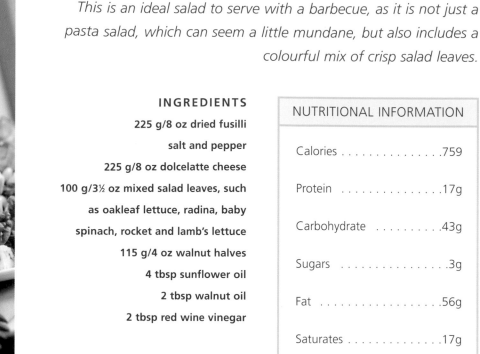

This is an ideal salad to serve with a barbecue, as it is not just a pasta salad, which can seem a little mundane, but also includes a colourful mix of crisp salad leaves.

INGREDIENTS

225 g/8 oz dried fusilli

salt and pepper

225 g/8 oz dolcelatte cheese

100 g/3½ oz mixed salad leaves, such

as oakleaf lettuce, radina, baby

spinach, rocket and lamb's lettuce

115 g/4 oz walnut halves

4 tbsp sunflower oil

2 tbsp walnut oil

2 tbsp red wine vinegar

NUTRITIONAL INFORMATION	
Calories 759	
Protein 17g	
Carbohydrate 43g	
Sugars 3g	
Fat 56g	
Saturates 17g	

cook's tip

You can substitute another piquant cheese for the dolcelatte, such as Stilton, goat's cheese or even feta, if you prefer.

1 Cook the pasta in a large saucepan of lightly salted boiling water for 8–10 minutes, or until tender, but still firm to the bite. Drain, rinse under cold running water and drain again.

2 Using a sharp knife, cut the dolcelatte cheese into cubes. Place the salad leaves in a large serving bowl and add the cooked pasta. Sprinkle the dolcelatte cheese on top.

3 Preheat the grill to medium. Place the walnut halves on a large baking tray and cook under the grill for a few minutes, or until lightly toasted. Leave to cool. Mix the sunflower oil, walnut oil and wine vinegar together in a jug and season to taste with salt and pepper. Pour the dressing over the salad, toss lightly, then top with the toasted walnuts.

red & green salad

cook: 5 mins   prep: 10 mins   serves 4

Beetroot and orange is a classic combination and here they are combined with tender, baby spinach leaves to make a dramatic and colourful warm salad.

NUTRITIONAL INFORMATION	
Calories	173
Protein	5g
Carbohydrate	20g
Sugars	18g
Fat	9g
Saturates	1g

INGREDIENTS

650 g/1 lb 7 oz cooked beetroot

3 tbsp extra virgin olive oil

juice of 1 orange

1 tsp caster sugar

1 tsp fennel seeds

salt and pepper

115 g/4 oz fresh baby spinach leaves

cook's tip

To cook beetroot, trim the leaves and rinse. Cook in a saucepan of salted water for 1 hour, or until tender. Drain and cool. Rub off the skin and trim the root.

1 Using a sharp knife, dice the cooked beetroot and reserve until required. Heat the olive oil in a small, heavy-based saucepan. Add the orange juice, sugar and fennel seeds and season to taste with salt and pepper. Stir constantly until the sugar has dissolved.

2 Add the reserved beetroot to the saucepan and stir gently to coat. Remove the saucepan from the heat.

3 Arrange the baby spinach leaves in a large salad bowl. Spoon the warmed beetroot on top and serve immediately.

desserts

Cooking desserts on the barbecue is not very common, perhaps because everyone is already full of grilled food, the cook is fed up with wielding the tongs or the barbecue grill is smothered with soy sauce or wholegrain mustard. This is rather a pity because many fruits acquire a new character when chargrilled.

A second barbecue will avoid the residues of savoury dishes. Most desserts cook quite quickly, so an inexpensive disposable barbecue would be perfectly satisfactory for recipes such as Totally Tropical Pineapple (see page 162) or Cinnamon Fruit with Chocolate Smoothie (see page 170). Alternatively, choose one of the recipes, such as Coconut Apples (see page 166), where the fruit is wrapped in foil before cooking.

If you are hot and bothered and never want to see a briquette again, try persuading another member of the family to take over cooking the dessert. Many desserts benefit from prolonged marinating, so you can prepare them in advance and let someone else turn and brush them.

Finally, have you considered serving a barbecued dessert at the end of a different kind of meal? For example, if you are entertaining guests to an alfresco lunch of cold dishes that you have made in advance, the barbecue can be heating up while you are eating the main course and you can then cook the dessert. This would make a delightful and unusual finale to the meal.

totally tropical pineapple

cook: 6–8 mins   **prep: 15 mins**   **serves 4**

NUTRITIONAL INFORMATION

Calories 206

Protein 1g

Carbohydrate 20g

Sugars 20g

Fat 12g

Saturates 7g

variation

If you prefer, you can cut the pineapple into cubes or quarters and thread on skewers before brushing with the rum mixture and cooking.

The delicious aroma of fresh pineapple and rum as this succulent, mouthwatering dessert is cooking will transport you to a Caribbean beach. The ground ginger adds just a touch of spice.

INGREDIENTS

1 pineapple

3 tbsp dark rum

2 tbsp muscovado sugar

1 tsp ground ginger

4 tbsp unsalted butter, melted

cook's tip

If possible, use a separate grill rack or even barbecue to cook the pineapple on. It is best to use a pair of long-handled tongs to turn the pineapple rings over while cooking.

1 Preheat the barbecue. Using a sharp knife, cut off the crown of the pineapple, then cut the fruit into 2-cm/¾-inch thick slices. Cut away the peel from each slice and flick out the 'eyes' with the point of the knife. Stamp out the cores with an apple corer or small pastry cutter.

2 Mix the rum, sugar, ginger and butter together in a jug, stirring constantly, until the sugar has dissolved. Brush the pineapple rings with the rum mixture.

3 Cook the pineapple rings over hot coals for 3–4 minutes on each side. Transfer to serving plates and serve immediately with the remaining rum mixture poured over them.

caramelized fruit

serves 4   **prep: 15 mins, plus 1 hr marinating**   **cook: 5 mins**

It is quite unusual to include fresh strawberries in a chargrilled fruit salad, but they work surprising well and taste delicious.

INGREDIENTS

150 ml/5 fl oz medium sherry

115 g/4 oz caster sugar

4 peaches

1 ogen melon, halved and deseeded

225 g/8 oz strawberries

NUTRITIONAL INFORMATION

Calories 234

Protein 2g

Carbohydrate 49g

Sugars 49g

Fat 0g

Saturates 0g

cook's tip

Choose large, ripe strawberries for this dish. Do not hull them and make sure that they are turned frequently during cooking to prevent burning.

1 Mix the sherry and sugar together in a large bowl, stirring constantly, until the sugar has dissolved.

2 Cut the peaches in half and remove the stones, then place in a bowl and cover with boiling water. Leave for 15–20 seconds, then remove with a slotted spoon. Peel off the skin. Cut the melon halves into wedges and cut the flesh away from the skin. Add the melon wedges, peach halves and strawberries to the sherry mixture, tossing gently to coat. Cover with clingfilm and leave to marinate in the refrigerator for 1 hour.

3 Preheat the barbecue. Drain the fruit, reserving the marinade. Cook the melon and peaches over hot coals for 3 minutes, then add the strawberries and cook for a further 2 minutes. Turn the fruit and brush frequently with the reserved marinade. Serve.

special peach melba

cook: 3–5 mins

prep: 15 mins, plus 1 hr marinating

serves 4

The elegant simplicity of this rich, fruity dessert makes it the perfect end to a special occasion barbecue party.

NUTRITIONAL INFORMATION	
Calories	.480
Protein	.8g
Carbohydrate	.83g
Sugars	.79g
Fat	.15g
Saturates	.10g

INGREDIENTS

2 large peaches, peeled, halved and stoned

1 tbsp light brown sugar

1 tbsp Amaretto liqueur

450 g/1 lb fresh raspberries, plus extra to decorate

115 g/4 oz icing sugar

600 ml/1 pint vanilla ice cream

cook's tip

For the best results, remove the vanilla ice cream from the freezer 20 minutes before serving and leave in the refrigerator. This allows it to soften slightly and makes it easier to scoop.

1 Place the peach halves in a large, shallow dish and sprinkle with the brown sugar. Pour the Amaretto liqueur over them, cover with clingfilm and leave to marinate for 1 hour.

2 Meanwhile, using the back of a spoon, press the raspberries through a fine sieve set over a bowl. Discard the contents of the sieve. Stir the icing sugar into the raspberry purée. Cover the bowl with clingfilm and leave to chill in the refrigerator until required.

3 Preheat the barbecue. Drain the peach halves, reserving the marinade. Cook over hot coals, turning and brushing frequently with the reserved marinade, for 3–5 minutes. To serve, put 2 scoops of vanilla ice cream in each of 4 sundae glasses, top with a peach half and spoon the raspberry sauce over it. Decorate with whole raspberries and serve.

coconut apples

serves 4   **prep: 10 mins**   **cook: 15–20 mins**

This is a barbecue variation of the ever-popular dessert of baked apples, but instead of being filled with dried fruit, they are layered with a rich combination of jam and coconut.

INGREDIENTS

2 tsp unsalted butter

4 tbsp ginger and apple jam

115 g/4 oz desiccated coconut

pinch of ground cinnamon

4 cooking apples

double cream or ice cream, to serve (optional)

NUTRITIONAL INFORMATION

Calories 312

Protein 2g

Carbohydrate 32g

Sugars 32g

Fat 20g

Saturates 17g

---

variation

You can substitute large, firm pears for the apples and use different flavoured jams, such as apricot.

cook's tip

Desiccated coconut is usually available from most large supermarkets and specialist food shops. Store in an airtight container and use it quickly.

1 Preheat the barbecue. Cut out 4 squares of kitchen foil, each large enough to enclose 1 apple, and lightly grease with the unsalted butter. Mix the ginger and apple jam and coconut together in a small bowl and stir in cinnamon to taste.

2 Core the apples, but don't peel them. Cut each apple horizontally into 3 slices. Spread the mixture between the apple slices and reassemble the apples. Place an apple on each sheet of foil and fold up the sides to enclose securely.

3 Cook the apples over hot coals for 15–20 minutes. Serve immediately with cream or ice cream, if you like.

mixed fruit kebabs

serves 4   **prep: 20 mins, plus** ⏲   **cook: 5–7 mins** ⏲
1 hr marinating

You can use almost any firm-fleshed fruit to make these colourful, quick and easy kebabs. Remember to soak the wooden skewers in cold water before using to prevent burning.

INGREDIENTS

2 nectarines, halved and stoned

2 kiwi fruit

4 red plums

1 mango, peeled, halved and stoned

2 bananas, peeled and thickly sliced

8 strawberries, hulled

1 tbsp clear honey

3 tbsp Cointreau

NUTRITIONAL INFORMATION

Calories 185

Protein 3g

Carbohydrate 38g

Sugars 37g

Fat 1g

Saturates 0g

cook's tip

If serving these kebabs to children, omit the Cointreau and use orange juice instead. It may be easier to remove the cooked fruit from the skewers before serving.

1 Cut the nectarine halves in half again and place in a large, shallow dish. Peel and quarter the kiwi fruit. Cut the plums in half and remove the stones. Cut the mango flesh into chunks and add to the dish with the kiwi fruit, plums, bananas and strawberries.

2 Mix the honey and Cointreau together in a jug until well blended. Pour the mixture over the fruit and toss lightly to coat. Cover with clingfilm and leave to marinate in the refrigerator for 1 hour.

3 Preheat the barbecue. Drain the fruit, reserving the marinade. Thread the fruit

on to several presoaked wooden skewers and cook over medium hot coals, turning and brushing frequently with the reserved marinade, for 5–7 minutes, then serve.

fruit parcels

cook: 4 mins **prep: 15 mins** **serves 4**

If you don't have a 'spare' barbecue, cooking fruit in a parcel is a good idea for dessert, as it avoids any contamination from earlier savoury courses and keeps the fruit wonderfully succulent.

NUTRITIONAL INFORMATION	
Calories	112
Protein	2g
Carbohydrate	28g
Sugars	28g
Fat	0g
Saturates	0g

INGREDIENTS

2 oranges

2 eating apples

juice of 1 lemon

2 pears

4 tsp muscovado sugar

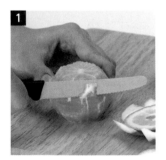

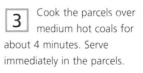

cook's tip

Brushing a little lemon juice on to cut fruit, such as apples and pears, prevents them from discolouring. It also enhances their flavour

1 Preheat the barbecue. Peel the oranges, carefully removing all the pith. Cut each orange horizontally into 6 slices. Core the apples, but do not peel. Cut each apple horizontally into 6 slices. Brush the slices with lemon juice. Peel and core the pears, then cut each of them horizontally into 6 slices. Brush the slices with lemon juice.

2 Cut out 4 large squares of foil. Divide the fruit slices equally between the squares and sprinkle each pile with 1 teaspoon of the sugar. Fold up the sides of the squares to enclose the fruit securely.

3 Cook the parcels over medium hot coals for about 4 minutes. Serve immediately in the parcels.

cinnamon fruit with chocolate smoothie

serves 4   **prep: 10 mins**   **cook: 10 mins**

Fresh fruit kebabs are coated with spicy butter before grilling and are then served with an easy-to-prepare, rich chocolate sauce.

INGREDIENTS

4 slices fresh pineapple

2 kiwi fruit, peeled and quartered

12 strawberries, hulled

1 tbsp melted unsalted butter

1 tsp ground cinnamon

1 tbsp orange juice

SMOOTHIE

225 g/8 oz plain chocolate

25 g/1 oz unsalted butter

125 g/4½ oz caster sugar

125 ml/4 fl oz evaporated milk

1 tsp vanilla essence

4 tbsp Kahlúa

NUTRITIONAL INFORMATION	
Calories	.643
Protein	.6g
Carbohydrate	.91g
Sugars	.88g
Fat	.29g
Saturates	.17g

cook's tip

Always try to find the best-quality chocolate that you can buy. Try to break the chocolate into pieces roughly the same size, so they will all melt at the same rate.

1 Preheat the barbecue. To make the smoothie, break the chocolate into pieces and melt with the butter in a saucepan over a low heat. Stir in the sugar and evaporated milk and cook, stirring, until the sugar has dissolved and the sauce has thickened. Transfer to a heatproof bowl and set on the side of the barbecue to keep hot.

2 Cut the pineapple slices into chunks. Thread the pineapple chunks, kiwi fruit and strawberries alternately on to several presoaked wooden skewers. Mix the butter, cinnamon and orange juice together in a small bowl. Brush the fruit kebabs all over with the cinnamon butter.

3 Cook the kebabs over hot coals, turning and brushing frequently with any remaining cinnamon butter, for 3–5 minutes, or until golden. Just before serving, stir the vanilla essence and Kahlúa into the smoothie.

stuffed pears

cook: 20 mins   **prep: 20 mins**   **serves 4**

It is a popular practice to sprinkle strawberries with pepper to bring out their flavour — this is equally effective with other fruit.

NUTRITIONAL INFORMATION	
Calories	184
Protein	1g
Carbohydrate	42g
Sugars	42g
Fat	3g
Saturates	2g

INGREDIENTS

2 tsp unsalted butter, for greasing

4 firm dessert pears

2 tbsp lemon juice

4 tbsp rosehip syrup

1 tsp green peppercorns,
lightly crushed

140 g/5 oz redcurrants

4 tbsp caster sugar

ice cream, to serve

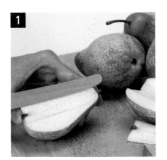

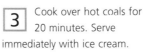

1 Preheat the barbecue. Cut out 4 squares of foil, each large enough to enclose the pears, and grease with the butter. Halve and core the pears, but do not peel. Brush the cut surfaces with lemon juice. Place 2 pear halves on each of the foil squares, brush them with the rosehip syrup and sprinkle with the peppercorns.

2 Place the redcurrants in a bowl and sprinkle with the sugar. Spoon the redcurrant mixture into the cavities of the pears. Fold up the sides of the foil to enclose the pears securely.

3 Cook over hot coals for 20 minutes. Serve immediately with ice cream.

cook's tip

When buying pears, always choose slightly underripe ones and allow them to ripen at room temperature. The best variety is Conference.

barbecued fruit with maple syrup

serves 4   **prep: 20 mins**   **cook: 10 mins**

*Slices of juicy fruit are coated in a rich maple syrup sauce as they
cook in little parcels on the barbecue.*

INGREDIENTS

1 papaya

1 mango, peeled and stoned

2 bananas

2 peaches, halved, stoned and peeled

1 ogen melon, halved and seeded

115 g/4 oz unsalted butter, diced

4 tbsp maple syrup

pinch of ground mixed spice

NUTRITIONAL INFORMATION

Calories 383

Protein 2g

Carbohydrate 42g

Sugars 40g

Fat 24g

Saturates 16g

cook's tip

Look for 'pure' or '100 per cent' maple syrup, which is quite expensive. Cheaper varieties may be blended with other types of syrup.

1 Preheat the barbecue. Cut out 4 large squares of foil. Using a sharp knife, cut the papaya in half and remove the seeds, then cut the halves into thick slices and peel off the skin. Thickly slice the mango and remove the stone, then peel off the skin and cut the flesh into slices. Peel the bananas and cut in half lengthways. Slice the peach

halves. Cut the melon halves into thin wedges, then cut the flesh away from the rind. Divide the fruit between the foil squares.

2 Put the butter and maple syrup into a food processor and process until thoroughly blended and smooth. Divide the flavoured butter between the parcels of

fruit and sprinkle with a little mixed spice. Fold up the sides of the foil to enclose the fruit securely.

3 Cook over medium hot coals, turning occasionally, for 10 minutes. Remove from the parcels and serve immediately.

banana sizzles

⏲ **cook: 6–8 mins**   ◔ **prep: 10 mins**   **serves 4**

Bananas are particularly sweet and delicious when grilled – and conveniently come with their own protective wrapping.

NUTRITIONAL INFORMATION	
Calories	.284
Protein	.2g
Carbohydrate	.41g
Sugars	.38g
Fat	.12g
Saturates	.8g

INGREDIENTS

3 tbsp butter, softened

2 tbsp dark rum

1 tbsp orange juice

4 tbsp muscovado sugar

pinch of ground cinnamon

4 bananas

orange zest, to decorate

1 Preheat the barbecue. Beat the butter with the rum, orange juice, sugar and cinnamon in a small bowl until thoroughly blended and smooth.

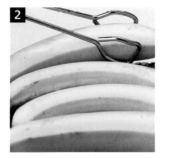

2 Place the bananas, without peeling, over hot coals and cook, turning frequently, for 6–8 minutes, or until the skins are blackened.

3 Transfer the bananas to serving plates, slit the skins and cut partially through the flesh lengthways. Divide the flavoured butter between the bananas, decorate with orange zest and serve.

cook's tip

Try cooking the bananas in foil. Cut them in half lengthways without peeling. Spread the butter over the cut surfaces and reassemble. Wrap in foil. Cook over medium hot coals for 5–10 minutes.

index